The Millionaire In Progress

How To Really Become Financially Free

Carlos Bermudez

Copyright © 2018 Carlos Bermudez

All Rights Reserved

To my mother, who always supported me and believed in me when no one else would. I love you.

TABLE OF CONTENTS:

The Process Has Begun – pg. 6

The Lion And The Gazelle – pg. 9

Your Thoughts Become Things – pg. 14

The Freedom Mentality – pg. 29

What To Expect In The Beginning – pg. 32

Close The Gap: Skip The Ladder And Take The Elevator – pg. 49

Why The Rich Get Richer And The Poor Get Poorer – pg. 64

Experiments Equal Success – pg. 79

The Twelve Decrees Of Money – pg. 84

The Phoenix – pg. 101

Do Me A Favor – pg. 106

The Process Has Begun

"A formal education will make you a living; but a self-education will make you a fortune." - Jim Rohn

Congratulations on taking your first step to becoming financially free! I also wanted to thank you for purchasing this book. It truly means so much to me that I can help guide you on this very important life decision. I know the idea of becoming rich beyond your wildest dreams feels more like a fantasy than a reality at the moment, but soon you'll come to realize that what you desire most is not so far away. There is hope. Your goal of becoming a free man or woman is only pages away. We all know that the gap between the haves and have-nots is growing and just affording to live is getting more expensive, but all that can change by raising your financial IQ and learning to make money work for you. No longer will you be a slave to bills, mortgages, car payments and debt. No longer will you be paid less than you are worth, but enough to keep crawling back to your job. You see, anyone can become financially free if they really want to. All it takes is knowing in your gut, deep down, that you deserve everything life has to offer. You deserve to have a bank account with more digits than any license plate. You deserve to travel the world and explore the exotic parts of it that you have only seen on Instagram posts. You deserve to have endless free time to spend with your loved ones. You deserve to own that house in Beverly Hills. You deserve to own that

Lamborghini. You were not born to pay bills the rest of your life and die a quiet death. You were born to enjoy the fruit of life. This book which you are currently holding in your hands was created for you. This book holds the answers you have been searching for. If you have been feeling stuck, held back, or lost, this book is your guide out of the darkness.

I've read many books on becoming wealthy. Each having its own golden nugget of wisdom waiting for the reader to take it straight out of its pages and apply it to their life, but I have yet to find a book that has smelt them together into a single golden ingot; until now. This book is that gold ingot. Should you choose to utilize this book in your endeavors of a new reality is completely up to you. The answers now rest in the palm of your hands.

The Lion and the Gazelle

When you woke up this morning what motivated you to get up out of your bed? Did you think about someone in particular that depends on you? Was it the fear of not going to work and running the risk of being fired? Was it not having enough money to pay your bills? Or was it the burning desire inside your heart to do great things with your life? Why do you do what you do? What is the reason you decided to buy this book? There are a lot of people who are not successful in life, not because they don't have the talent, skills, or potential, but because the reason behind their purpose is weak. The reason why you struggle to wake up at 5AM, the reason why you give up after a month, the reason why you don't work that extra hour, read that extra chapter, do that extra something is because you don't have that motive that is pushing the action. Before you embark on this journey of becoming financially free, it is critical to your success that you prepare yourself by digging deep down and asking yourself why you are doing this. Who is it that you want to become? What is it you deserve?

You must lay down a foundation with enough fortitude to withstand the multiple obstacles, setbacks, and failures Life will throw at you. Yes, there are many days full of sunshine ahead of you, but a number of rainy days, weeks, or sometimes even months await you, too. It is not a matter of IF it will happen, but a matter of WHEN and your *why* must be strong enough to withstand life's wildcards. It's time you look inside yourself and decide that YOU are in charge of your destiny. Not your teacher, your friends your parents, or significant other. It's time to face yourself in the mirror and ask yourself what reason do you have to succeed.

For some of you it will be not having to go back to that terrible workplace and deal with the low pay, work drama, and lack of fun that unfortunately comes with your job. For others it will be wanting to have the freedom to travel the world and see every beautiful location this wonderful planet has to offer. To be able to stand at the summit of a certain mountain and scream "I did it." To spend hours lying on the warm sand only to hear the crashing of waves in the not so far distance. Can you feel the warm sand under your feet and hear the waves? Maybe you want to buy the finest luxuries on the market today and be able to wear the newest fashion down Rodeo Drive in Los Angeles, California. Can you see yourself walking down Rodeo Drive wearing only the best? Your reason could be that you have a passion for cars and want to have your garage full of exotics. Can you hear the sound of that V12 engine revving?

Whatever the case may be, your *why* should be able to propel you forward and inspire you whenever life has you up against the ropes. Your *why* should be self-affirmed every single day when you wake up. When you are in the shower. When you are in the car driving anywhere and everywhere. When you are stuck in your own thoughts. When your anxiety starts to get the best of you. When you have lost all your money. When you have secluded yourself in your room, crying into your pillow because of how overwhelmed you are. When you can't see the light at the end of the tunnel.

Your *why* will be that game changer. It will be the beaming lighthouse continuously beaconing your way through the treacherous storm. It will be the constant reminder motivating you to keep moving forward no matter what. That's what separates the losers from the winners.

Your *why* will remind you that you are fighting for your own freedom. Your *why* will push you to overcome every obstacle that has been placed on your path. Your *why* will be the truth exposing the many false beliefs the word "impossible" has tainted over the history of mankind. Your *why* should be forged by faith because there will come a time when your *why* will truly be tested.

When you get to the point where you feel really stuck. When you get to the point where it hurts really bad. When you get to the point where enough is enough. When you get to the point where you've depleted all your money. When you can't take it anymore. When you get to that point, doors start opening and opportunities will begin to appear, but only if you keep going just a little further. What you cannot do is quit during the process. You cannot give up or give in. Winners keep going when they have nothing left in their tank. When they have no more energy. When they have hit rock bottom. When you have spent your last dollar. When you look around and nowhere do you see success. That's when your *why* will remind you that you are fighting for your own freedom.

If you have tried time after time but somehow always find yourself coming up short or not having the energy or motivation to keep going, it is because your *why* just wasn't strong enough. What happens when your *why* isn't strong enough? You become a gazelle. You are a gazelle. A gazelle constantly needs something external to motivate it. What happens to the gazelle when the lion isn't chasing it? What happens is nothing. The gazelle stops running. Why? Because the gazelle always needs something external to motivate it. Stop being the gazelle. You are in charge of your own destiny. Find your purpose; the reason to be alive on this planet. It's time you become the lion and go after your dreams as if your life depends on it. If the lion does not hunt the gazelle, the lion does not eat nor does it survive. It's that simple. Find your *why*.

Your Thoughts Become Things

Religions such as Islam, Judaism, Christianity, Hinduism, and Buddhism have used it in their teachings. Great men that have been immortalized by engraving their names into history itself, Socrates, Plato, Aristotle, Sir Isaac Newton, William Shakespeare, Leonardo Da Vinci, Andrew Carnegie, Henry Ford, Theodore Roosevelt, Woodrow Wilson, Thomas A. Edison, Martin Luther King Jr., and many more, have used this powerful universal law to their advantage in the growth of their legacy. The jewel of the ancient world, Babylonia, grew to its legendary status by using this law as its foundation to acquire its great wealth. Not only was it prosperous financially, but its citizens had the most valuable wisdom correlated to the science of acquiring gold. It is a law that has been named one of the natural laws of our universe. I am of course talking about the all-powerful Law of Attraction.

All things that have come into your life were not placed there by sheer coincidence. With or without your knowledge, you are to credit or blame for everything that has become part of your life. People, opportunities, problems, and materialistic matter. They have all attracted to you because of the thoughts you hold within your conscious and subconscious mind. It doesn't matter who you are or what you are doing. Your thoughts and the images you hold in your mind have been forming the life around you this whole time.

For as long as man could desire, their success has been drawn to them through their thoughts, consciously and subconsciously. Every successful man and woman that you have ever heard about or seen somewhere, that was not born with a silver spoon in their mouth, had to start somewhere; Their mind. They had to envision it before it was a reality. You see, when all you think about is the abundance of wealth and only the existence of wealth, without allowing contradictory thoughts of doubt to stem within your mind, you are creating and transmitting a sort of vibe or signal from your thoughts. That signal is sent out into the universe. The universe then reacts to this signal by creating a natural balance. If you do not yet have an abundance of wealth, yet your dominant thoughts are envisioning a reality in which you already have an abundance of riches, the universe will move, bend, and place that which you have envisioned and believed to be real, into your life.

For example, have you ever thought about something that made you upset, and the more you thought about it the worse the situation became? Even getting to the point where the outcome scenarios you have created in your head, because of how worried you were, became a reality? That's because you filled your mind with negative thoughts, transmitting a signal and using the law of attraction to bring forth more *like* scenarios. The law will always respond to your thoughts, no matter what they might be. You must constantly be aware of what you are thinking consciously and subconsciously. Whatever you think about, you will attract.

Whatever you do, you will attract. Whatever you are, you will attract. The human mind constantly emits signals that act as a powerful magnet attracting whatever thoughts dominate your mind. Through this powerful law, your thoughts will become your life. If you are not happy with your life, it is because your life is a reflection of your past thoughts and has been comprised of what they have attracted. Since you attract what you think about most, it's very clear to see why you are where you are. If you constantly think and say that you are broke, you will become broke. If you constantly think and say that making money is very hard, then it will become very hard to make money. If you think and say that there is no way of you becoming financially stable or become rich beyond your wildest dreams due to the hand life has dealt you, then you will never know the taste of true freedom.

If you wish to change your life, then you must change your thoughts. You must learn to self-affirm positive thoughts over and over. You must hold onto the thoughts you want most and repeat thinking of them every day. By doing so you become what you most think about and attract what you think about most. Begin to envision yourself in terms of success. Whatever your definition of success might be. Make it very clear as to what a successful version of yourself looks like. Now envision what a successful version of yourself looks like in 3, 5, 10, 20 years ahead of now and the steps it took you to get there. Imagine it so clearly that you can believe it is your reality. Then, believe it to be your own destiny. Start taking actions in the direction of your visions. Begin to think and act like the successful version of yourself. Begin to study and learn what the successful version of yourself is already a master of. Begin to connect and build rapport with the people you envision the successful version of yourself has healthy relationships and partnerships with. Begin to take actions toward becoming the successful version of yourself in order to become it. By deliberately producing positive thoughts and taking correlated actions, you will begin to emit signals into the universe. Your job is to hold onto these thoughts and continue doing those actions. Although change may not be instant, you must continue to do it every day thereon forward and believe in the law. There are many real-life examples of the powerful Law of Attraction. I will be sharing only three of them today with you.

 Jim Carrey was born on January 17, 1962, in Newmarket Ontario Canada and was the youngest of four siblings. His father, Percy, was a jazz performer turned bookkeeper in order provide for his family. Although his family struggled financially in the beginning, it wasn't enough to stop Jim from believing he could make his dreams of becoming a comedic movie star a reality. His desire to become one of the greats transmitted into the universe, allowing the law to attract that which me wanted most. At age 19, Carrey decided to head out to Hollywood, but like many young actors trying to become successful there, he found that success was difficult to achieve. Although he had found opportunities at comedy clubs, his movie deals were not yet a part of his reality. That was something the law needed some time for.

 He would spend his days thinking about what it would be like to star in a blockbuster hit. To have his name known throughout the country as one of the funniest in the business. He was constantly imagining what it would be like to not struggle financially anymore and finally become free.

This went on for quite some time until he stumbled across and learned about the Law of Attraction. Learning more about it he decided to give it a chance. In 1985, a broke and depressed Carrey drove his old beat-up Toyota up the Hollywood hills. Once he was there, in order to make himself feel better, Carrey wrote himself a check for ten million dollars for "acting services rendered," and post-dated it 10 years into the future and kept it in his wallet.

Jim carried that check everywhere he went. It was a subtle reminder of the law and his responsibility to think about the reality he wanted. The check remained there until it deteriorated. 10 years passed and Carey still never lost sight of what he wanted most out of life. Then something happened. A little after the tenth anniversary of writing the check, he was written a real check for ten million dollars for a movie that turned out to be a blockbuster hit. After that, Carrey earned millions for movies like *Ace Ventura: Pet Detective* and *Dumb and Dumber*. When his father passed away in 1994, Carrey slipped the check in the casket to be buried. Feel free to look up the interview on Jim Carrey by Oprah on YouTube.

The Second example of the Law of Attraction is one many of you will resonate with. A topic many struggled with but have found it has touched a part of their lives in some way or another. There was a man who was part of an elite military group only a few will ever become eligible for. A group made up of men with the extraordinary mental resilience and fortitude to withstand the toughest military training on the planet. They conduct covert missions around the world, one being the successful termination of Osama Bin Laden, on May 2, 2011. These men have earned the title of

Navy SEALs. Although they may seem invincible, they are not immune to developing illnesses. A SEAL Team member coming home from leave had been keeping track of a weird one-inch rigid mass developing on his abdomen for the last two months. Although he wasn't experiencing any pain, his concern began to slowly grow as the mass wasn't fading away. Having his health in his best interest, he decided to get himself medically examined as soon as he had the opportunity to do so. He grabbed his phone and skimmed through his contacts until he came across the phone number of the closest VA hospital to his home. He was hoping to set up an appointment for the following morning.

The man pressed the green "call" button near his thumb as soon as the number appeared on the screen. A couple rings into the call a soft voice began introducing itself. As he explained his concern for the mass developing in his abdomen, the now gentle-voiced women on the other end of the call began typing away. "...OK, Doctor Michaels will see you tomorrow morning!"

The sun was shining in through the passenger side of the car window reflecting off the man's eyes that morning as he drove in the direction of the illuminated horizon. In the driver's seat was his wife. The ride thus far had been very quiet for fear that a single word of doubt escaping either of their mouths would inevitably seal their future for the worse. They both tried to keep hope and optimism on the surface of their mind, but it was hard to deny the elephant in the room had put them on a path to open Pandora's Box. Upon arrival, they got out of the car, walked into the waiting room and filled out required paperwork to be seen by Dr. Michaels. The only option now was to wait patiently and not lose control of their positive thinking to negative thoughts that could be caused by their anxiety and fear of the unknown. As they both looked at each other, it was clear they were players participating in a waiting game. Time felt like an eternity just sitting there.

    The door finally opened and a young lady simultaneously called out the man's name while signaling them to come in through the door. Holding each other's hands, they both followed the nurse to the triage room and sat down in their respective area. It wasn't long before Dr. Michaels had entered the room, introduced himself, and recommend to start tests in order to identify the cause of the mass. As the day went on and testing came to an end, the man and his wife were eager to have an answer. Unfortunately, they would have to wait a couple days for the tests to be analyzed and be given results.

    A few days later, the man's cell phone began to buzz as an incoming call came through. The man answered by giving a friendly greeting and responded to Dr. Michaels on the other end of the phone call. "We have your results and we're going to need you to come in and review them together. Are you able to make it in today?" Said Dr. Michaels. "Yes. I can be in the office in about an hour," the man replied. He went back inside his home and called out to his wife in order to inform her of the phone call. They both finished up what they were doing, gathered their things, and went on their way to the hospital. When they arrived, the front desk secretary asked them to wait momentarily while

Dr. Michaels finished up with his last patient. She directed them into a room to sit and wait for the doctor.

Minutes later, there were two knocks on the door before it was opened. Both the man and women's face directed their attention towards the opening door. As Dr. Michaels walked into the room avoiding any eye contact, he wore a distinct guilty face as to allude bad news. During the time Dr. Michaels had entered the room and sat down in front of his computer typing away on his keyboard, not a single word had been spoken from anyone. The man and his wife sat on the edge of their seats waiting for words to escape Dr. Michaels mouth. "I'm glad you were able to make it on such a short notice. I know this matter has been of a concern to you so I wanted to make sure I spoke with you in person. The analyses were sent back this morning and I told my tech to place it on my desk so I could review it myself. Now, I'm going to give you enough time to process this so feel free to ask me anything you want to know. It appears the rigid mass in your abdomen is a malignant tumor that has been developing for some time now. Unfortunately, this is a rare type of cancer that hasn't been explored in depth yet. Now, there are some experimental drugs we could test and other possible treatments like chemotherapy, but we can discuss that when you're ready." Dr. Michaels said. He then sat on his stool quietly as he knew there needed to be some processing done by the couple sitting in front of him.

No words came out from either of their mouths. Tears slowly began to slide down the women's cheek as she began to ask how it was possible for him to develop cancer when none of their ancestors had ever developed cancer themselves. She continued to ask more questions, but the sound of her voice was beginning to get drowned out into the background as the man became trapped in his thoughts. How was it that he had evaded death in some of the world's deadliest places, survived being pinned down by terrorist gunfire, yet ultimately was going to be defeated from an enemy within. "There has to be a way." he said. The room became quiet and both Dr. Michaels and the women were now staring at him. "There has to be a way to defeat it." he said. "Unfortunately, this cancer has a survivability rate of 2%. The only thing we can do is buy you a little bit more time. Perhaps you should start to prepare your family for the future." said Dr. Michaels. After the man heard what the doctor suggested, an urge of anger rose from within his chest. "How could you ask me to give up when there is still a chance of surviving this?" he said. "My whole life I've made sure to omit the words "" Give up" from my vocabulary and now you want me to accept them as if it's my only option? There's no way in hell I'm going down without a fight. I can beat this."

    Dr. Michaels understood and appreciated the man's will to fight back, but ultimately underestimated his chance of victory due to the survival rate of the type of cancer. "I understand you don't want to accept or believe it, but you have to start thinking of your family and how you'll want to prepare them for the future," Dr. Michaels said. "How long does he have?" the women said breaking her silence. "It's hard to tell because the tumor has been developing for quite some time now... From what I've heard of the other cases, I'd say he has no more than four months." Silence once again took over the room for what felt like minutes. "No. I can beat this." the man said. The doctor replied, "Look I understand you want to fight this but I don't think...," and was abruptly interrupted by the man one last time, "Watch me." Those were his last words before he grabbed his wife by the hand and left the office. The man did not accept this as is fate. He didn't care what the odds were, he only knew he'd beaten the odds before and believed he could do it again.

Over the next four months the only thing the man focused on was surviving the odds and proving he could overcome anything he set his mind to. His will to not give up and beat this cancerous mass was all he thought of. He imagined what his life would be like knowing he was one of the only people to survive and spend the rest of his days with his family. Every chance he could, he would envision himself hearing the very words "Congratulations, the cancer has disappeared." He self-affirmed this to himself over and over every morning when he went on his routinely runs. The man even had a whiteboard on the wall of his office where he had written in big lettering "I will be a survivor," in order to surround himself with the reality he believed in. With the support of his wife and family, the man would go on to take experimental drugs and participate in chemotherapy sessions. He did whatever he could do to fight back. For him there was no giving up. There was no failing. He knew deep inside him that he would succeed. His envisions got to the point where they started to feel like they had become previews of what was ahead of him. That brought a smile to his face. His beliefs now revolved around him surviving.

The days came and passed; the sun rose and set. Although Dr. Michaels had only given the man about four months to live, today marked the first day of the fifth month. The man and his wife had set up an appointment with Dr.

Michaels to examine the man's progress in his fight against the cancerous mass. Shortly after arriving into the waiting room, Dr. Michaels had happily invited them into his personal office. The man and wife both situated themselves in different chairs facing the doctor across his desk. On the desk was a white file with the man's name stamped on the top right corner of it. "These are your most recent results from the analytical tests we conducted last week. I thought it'd be better if both of you were present for the opening of it." said Dr. Michaels as he began pull one of the corners and tear open the file. Inside were documents with graphs and writing on them. As Dr. Michaels reviewed the results, a smile began to stretch from one corner of his face to the other.

      This was it. Every self-affirmation, every envision, every action had led him to this very point in time. When he had many reasons to accept his end and give up, he said to himself that there was a way. There is always a way. The man was now looking at Dr. Michaels ready to hear what he had to say. With a great big smile, Dr. Michaels looked at the man straight in his eyes and said, "Congratulations, your cancer has disappeared."

      Another example of The Law of Attraction is a personal one of mine. About a year ago I was working for a private ambulance company where I was constantly on the road going from hospital to hospital transporting patients. A sort of medical Uber if you will. It was certainly a job where the cons outweighed the pros. The cons were, but weren't limited to, being subjected to possible diseases, contaminated blood or bodily fluids, continuously dealing with misbehaved patients, being responsible for multiple lives when being behind the wheel of the ambulance, being held over for hours at a time all whilst being paid eleven dollars per hour. To me there were a lot more cons than pros, but there was something great about having to drive from hospital to hospital and that was getting to travel on the highway. Why was the highway so great? The highway was a place where exotic cars were given the chance to live up to their purpose, and that meant going really fast.

     Driving on the highway gave me multiple opportunities to see exotic cars and if you know me personally you know I love cars. I saw my first Ferrari, Lamborghini, McLaren, and Maserati on the highway. They were all amazing in their own way but there was something so beautiful and mesmerizing about that chrome trident on the front of a Maserati that truly captivated me. After seeing my first Maserati I started imagining what it would be like to drive one. Day in and day out I would picture myself sitting behind the steering wheel and feeling the pull back as my foot pressed the gas pedal to the floor. Even just thinking about myself getting to the point of owning one gave me goosebumps and brought a permanent smile to my face that would last the rest of the day. Now, at the time I was driving a 1997 Ford Ranger XLT so being able to drive a Maserati would have been such a huge upgrade. Even though my bank account said otherwise, I began to believe that it was possible for me to own a Maserati. I felt as if I already knew I was going to be the owner of a Maserati and it was just a matter of time before the universe placed it in front of me. This belief went on for about two weeks until I decided it was time to ditch the 1997 Ford Ranger XLT and buy myself a different car. I went online to a used cars website and started searching for used cars in my area. I came across a couple different options but I felt that I still hadn't found the perfect replacement. That's when my memory kicked into gear and reminded me of this belief I had clung onto so tightly. My curiosity asked to see if there were any used Maserati's for sale, even though logic said most used Maserati's could only be priced around sixty thousand dollars. I clicked on the Maserati tab then selected to show listings from least expensive to most expensive and BAM. There it was. A gorgeous silver Maserati coupe with a red leather interior within my budget and it was the only one. When I saw the listing, I knew this was the car I was going to own. This was the car I believed would be mine for the past two weeks. By imagining myself sitting behind the wheel of a Maserati and believing I would be the owner of it, I consciously transmitted into the universe what I wanted most and had used the law of attraction. I immediately called the dealership providing the listing and told them I wanted to go to the dealership and personally look at the car. I made the appointment to go the very next day at around 2:00PM.

  The next day, the drive was about an hour away from where I lived to get to the dealership. When I arrived and the car was parked, I began walking towards the front of the building where the entrance was. As I approached the entrance, I noticed that the Maserati was parked right by the entrance. Now that I was only inches away from the car, a sense of burning desire rose from within my chest. It was a strong feeling of attraction. I felt as if I was being magnetically pulled towards the driver's seat of the vehicle. I needed to be behind the wheel in order to create natural balance. The Universe had finally brought us together.

An hour later I drove off the dealership lot behind the wheel of a car. Only this time I wasn't driving the Ranger. I was driving the car I was meant to drive. I was driving the car I deserved to drive. The reality I had envisioned had come into fruition by simply using my thoughts. By instilling the Law of Attraction into my life, I had revolutionized my destiny forever. Now it's your turn. Your future reality begins and ends with your thoughts. Think wisely.

The Freedom Mentality

Now that your thoughts and heart are in the right place, it's time to act on it. Visualization will allow you to immerse yourself in a future you define as being successful, but it will also allow you to feel comfortable in newer situations. We as people can become very stressed when getting out of our comfort zones. There is a certain anxiety that goes along with trying new experiences that usually keeps us from moving forward in life. But I have great news. By visualizing yourself already doing whatever it is you need to do, it will allow you to transition easier moving forward. I say this because it is time you begin to build the foundation to your success and it all starts with your mentality. Your mentality plays a huge role in the creation of a better future.

You now know the secret of the Law of Attraction and its power but desiring alone won't be enough. You have to begin sculpting the right mentality in order to understand, strategize, and prepare for this game we call life. It's a game designed to weed out the uneducated and impatient, so you better start preparing yourself. Remember that there are no shortcuts, so there's no reason to feel rushed. I get it though, you want to be successful now, but that's not how it works. If you continue to have this rushed mentality, the only thing you will be doing is causing harm to your wellbeing. It will constantly feel like you are stuck in the mud and not going anywhere. You will begin look at the progress of others and question yourself on what it is you are doing wrong or different. You will begin to feel the weight of the world on your shoulders and slowly sink into a black abyss of depression. Shortly after that, all this negative energy will leak into the rest of your life and you will quit. Do not set yourself up for this trap. Why do you need that new house or car this very instance? Too many of us fall under this sort of thought process where we ask and wonder if I put in all this work, then what's in it for me right now. This isn't a 100-meter dash nor is it your typical 5k. This is much greater than that. Your journey is much greater than that. You have to fall in love with the process of your journey and focus on what you are becoming.

You are a passionate red Ferrari, hand crafted and designed to embark on this extraordinary epic adventure, for what will come to be known as "the most beautiful race in the world." Italians had something similar to this in 1926 called "The Mille Miglia," which translates to the "Thousand Miles" race. Your journey will consist of these thousand miles. Conquering them won't take a few days of work, it will take much more time than that. Remember that great things take time to grow, for it is only the farmer that faithfully plants seeds in the Spring, who reaps a harvest in the Fall.

Many of you are stressed thinking it's too late and yet most of you are between the ages of 25 and 40. It's never too late. You may be 50 years-old reading this but understand that this is as young as you'll ever be moving forward, so start now.

What To Expect In The Beginning

This portion of the book is so important that I wanted to make sure I delivered it to you before we continued any further. Consider this chapter your heads up and a fair warning. Now that you have decided to veer off the common path, you will notice a lot will change with that decision. I'm not just talking about it from a financial standpoint, but from a social one. Once you begin making more money than your friends, family, and the people around you in general, you'll start to see a shift in relationships and the way you are perceived. You will be judged and carry the stigma that you're some rich jerk simply because you are wearing a certain brand, drive a certain type of car, and make a certain amount of income. No one will sympathize with you when things turn for the worse. After all, you still have a lot of money. Even if money is not the only thing that matters to you in life, that's still what people will think of you. You will be expected to pay whenever you go out to eat with friends or family. You will always feel pressured to give handouts because people will tell you that they were part of the reason you are where you are now. People will say you're not worthy of the money and will remind you of how your past experiences and decisions define "who you really are." Many people will hate you for no other reason than your income and will try to convince the mass that your wealth has been acquired and handed down to you by your parents. Old acquaintances will appear out of nowhere and try to appeal to you in order to get close to your money. You may also be the target of crime if you make yourself a target. So please, be careful not to flaunt your wealth. Karma likes her scale of justice.

Although you may not experience all of these scenarios I've listed above, you are prone to experience a lot of them throughout your journey. They are all very real experiences that happen every day with upcoming wealthy people. As you fight this uphill battle, the one thing you'll constantly hear is people underestimating you. You will constantly be told "You won't make it," and be negatively reminded of how much you've changed. Here are two of my personal experiences that occurred to me at the very beginning of my journey and I'd like to share them with you.

The first time it was proved to me that people change on you was when I was twenty years old. I remember I was over at a friend's house with a couple of people and we were all hanging out in the basement sitting on a couch. I was on the very end of the couch because there was a power outlet and I needed it to charge my phone. All of the attention from the people sitting around me was being directed towards the television screen on the opposite side of the room. I believe they were watching a movie while I was on my phone. The reason I wasn't focusing on the movie was because at that time in my life I had recently been introduced to FOREX. Now, if you are not familiar with FOREX, I encourage you to learn about trading seeing as how millionaires are created everyday by simply trading foreign currencies. I use the word "simply" extremely lightly seeing as how you could lose all your money in one bad trade if you do not know what it is you are doing. Just like Warren Buffett says, "Risk comes from not knowing what you are doing." That's something I'll get into later in this book. Anyways, there I was sitting at the end of the couch, on my phone, not paying attention to the movie, in a room of friends. What was I doing on my phone you may ask? Well, I was in the middle of a trade. I don't quite remember which two currencies I was trading, but what I do remember was how excited I was when I multiplied my money. This was the first time I had ever made my money work for me instead of me work for my money. I saw the market becoming bearish so I decided to enter a sell trade at thirty cents. Slowly the market started to plummet, and with it my thirty cents became eleven dollars. When I saw that, I immediately closed the trade out of fear of losing that money and exited with a profit of eleven dollars. I was filled with so much joy and excitement afterwards that I started showing and telling everyone in the room that I had made my money work for me by turning thirty cents into eleven dollars! And I had done this all from my phone while I sat on the couch! I'm pretty sure I looked crazy from their perspective, but I wasn't thinking about that in the moment. What I was thinking about was if I could turn thirty cents into eleven dollars, imagine what I could do with one thousand dollars?

  Here I was on top of cloud nine feeling like I had finally figured out a way to gain my freedom, when all of a sudden, I saw the movie pause. Out of the corner of my eyes I could tell that I was being stared down by the friend whose house we were at. As I turned my head in her general direction, I could see her get up off the couch and walk towards me. What she said to me next is something I will never forget. She stood right in front of me, looked at me straight in my eyes and said, "Are you fucking serious? All you ever do is think about money. I hate this new you. What happened to the old Carlos? You've changed so much and I hate it." Now, this was a friend of mine that I had previously had a conversation with just a few days before this night and had asked her what her goals in life were out of pure curiosity. Her answer was that she wanted to marry a great guy, raise a family together, and be a school teacher for the rest of her life. She said that would be enough for her to be happy. To me that sounded great, and I was happy to hear she had goals to strive for that would bring her happiness. I then proceeded to ask her how she felt about her finances in the future and she answered, "Money doesn't matter to me as long as I have my family." At this point I tried to understand and see it through her point of view, but the idea that money wasn't necessary in her future conflicted with the idea of being free to do what she wanted to do most, and that was spend as much time with her family as she possibly could. Trying to sound understanding I then said, "Okay I see what you mean, but what if you could become financially free to the point where money wasn't a worry anymore? What if you had earned the freedom to do whatever it is you wanted most? For example, spend all of that free time with your family and be able to go on vacations as often as you wanted? One of the biggest reasons families fall apart is due to financial problems. Money isn't everything, but what it does offer is freedom and security." Before I could say anything else she interrupted me and told me again that she didn't care about money, and whatever I said wasn't going to change her view on it. So, in a way I guess I could say that I should have seen this coming sooner or later.

Going back to that night, after she told me that I had changed so much, she then proceeded to demand that I needed to change back to the person I was two years prior to that night. She kept repeating herself saying I had to change back to the person I once was when we had had first met. The only major problem with that was there was no way I could possibly, and willingly, return to something I had evolved from. Everyone in the room could feel the tension was rising. After what felt like a minute of silence, I asked her to elaborate on why she felt this way about me. Why did I need to change back to the person I once was? She told me that she didn't like the fact that all I had thought about for the past couple of weeks was money. She said the thought of someone being this greedy was so ugly and wouldn't plan on keeping them as a friend. In other words, the ultimatum was I either change back to who I was that made it more comfortable to be around, or she was going to stop being my friend all together. I told her there was no way I could go back to who I was because the old me from two years ago was so immature and irresponsible with money. She needed to understand that I wasn't going to change who I was just because it made her feel uncomfortable whenever she was around me. She either needed to accept me for who I was and what I believed in, or she didn't and we could end this so-called friendship right then and there.

When she heard this come out of my mouth, it was as if she was shocked that I had truly believed this. "How could you care more about money than your friends?" she would say. My response would always be the same; "I don't think money is the end all be all, but I do want to become financially free. I don't just think about money. I think about how I'm tired of working for it." She then said, "That's so stupid! That's just you being greedy and I'm not going to support that. Why does it even matter if you have to work for your money? My family has always worked for their money and they're fine" I then continued with, "I'm trying to become financially free because I am tired of living a paycheck to paycheck life. I hate the fact that I am paid less than I am worth, but enough to keep me crawling back to my job due the fact that I have to pay my bills. I'm not saying I won't be fine in the future if I continue to work for my money like your family has, but that's not what I want to do. I'm just tired of being an employee and having to work for someone else that doesn't really care about whether I have enough to pay my bills at the end of the month or not. All they really care about is making sure I come into work and make them more money. That may be okay for some people in this world, but that is not the life I want to live. I know I was born to do much more than just pay bills the rest of my life and then die."

  This type of back and forth went on for hours believe it or not. It went well into the night when she had pulled my best friend and I into a more soundproof room to continue speaking with me. By that time there were only three of us left. The reason she did this was because it had gotten so late that she didn't want to wake up her parents at 1:00am. In the middle of the room was a wooden table with six chairs and I sat on one end of the table while she sat across from me. My best friend sat to my left. Once we were all situated, she continued to ask me why I cared so much about becoming financially free and why it mattered so much to me in the first place. The problem with her repeatedly asking me these questions was that no matter how many times I explained it to her or tried to help her understand, she just wasn't going to get it. It wasn't just because she was stubborn, she also had a different outlook on life. She didn't have the same mentality I did. She was okay with the fact that for the rest of her life she would have to work for her money seeing as how that was normal to her. She was fine with working forty plus hours a week and living a simple life because that's exactly what she told me.

I'm not saying what she wanted to do in life was a bad choice or anything, all I'm saying is I accepted the fact that that's what she wanted out of her life. The problem here was she didn't accept what I wanted out of my life. She was mistaking my aspirations for greed and lack of values. She made it very clear that she thought I was wrong for ever thinking about wanting to become financially free. She continuously tried to persuade me to think I was wrong for what I was doing because in her eyes it wasn't "normal." Needless to say, she became very irritated after hours of trying to convince me and getting nowhere.

After another hour of being in that room, we heard some knocking coming from the door. Our attention was quickly drawn to the entrance of the room and to our surprise it was her dad coming in. He then looked at his daughter with a confused look on his face probably asking himself why we were still up at 2:00am. "Why are you awake, Dad?" she said. He then proceeded to say that the reason he was awake was due to hearing his daughter speak loudly. (By the way, people think you'll understand their opinion better by simply yelling it at you. We all know that doesn't work)

She replied to her dad by explaining the situation to him and expressing her opinion on why I needed to change back to the person she felt most comfortable being around. Stating that the person I wanted to be was "evil." To my surprise, after she had finished explaining the situation to him, he found himself siding with what his daughter had to say and her opinion. One would think he would have explained to her on why she should be able to accept others for who they are and what they want to do instead of trying to change their mentality. Instead he pulled up a chair and began to question me too. He asked me questions like, "Why do you care so much about becoming financially free?" and "Why do you even want to be like those rich assholes that only think about themselves?" He would then go on to say, "You do realize those types of people don't care about their family or friends." Again, I found myself explaining why I thought it was important to become financially literate and how I only had good intentions. I assured them that money wasn't going to change my morals, nor was I going to fall into the stereotype of the "rich douchebag." Unfortunately, he wasn't too fond of what I had to say seeing as how he once had a bad experience with someone close to him who had become wealthy growing up. Her dad told me he felt sorry for me forever thinking I needed money to become free. He said I was stupid for spending my time reading all these business books and claimed that they were more than likely a scam. When I heard that I simply stood up and left the house. I got into my car, drove home, and that was the end of that friendship. I wasn't going to sit there and have her cynical family criticize me for following my dreams.

Am I upset about what happened that night? Yes, of course. In all honesty I'm more disappointed in how it all played out. Especially knowing that my intentions were only positive. Because this was the first time I had experienced anything like this, it took me awhile to realize that this was going to be a recurring thing in my life. Not everyone is going to agree with my decisions or how I want to live my life and that's okay. You as the reader must understand that not everyone in your life will support what you are doing because it strays away from the norm. Some people may even work against you to make sure you never accomplish your dreams. With that said, you must be conscience of who you tell your dreams and aspirations to. For example, I don't recommend going into work one day and telling your coworkers that you're tired of working bullshit hours for bullshit pay and how you are planning to find a way to create passive income in order to quit your job. One of those coworkers you trust is bound to tell management or the owner of the establishment and they will make sure to honor your wishes by firing you then and there. Learn to work in silence and don't let your excitement get the best of you.

Fast forward a couple months down the road from that particular night. I had just started working as a car salesman in Highland Park, Illinois. I thought it would be in my best interest to work there because I wanted to practice my sales skills. What ended up happening was not only did my sales skills get sharper, but I learned so much about the power of credit, time management, and working with banks. Working there also put me in another scenario that I think you need to hear about.

When I started working at the dealership, I had to learn everything about the cars I was going to sell. That included online certification training provided by the car manufacturer and inhouse training. The way this dealership did inhouse training was by outsourcing it. Ironic right? The general manager at the dealership had hired his old boss and mentor that had shown him "the ropes" of selling cars some fifteen odd years ago. For privacy reasons, we'll call the inhouse trainer Jerry. He was very old school. Now, Jerry came into the dealership every Tuesday and Thursday to talk about his experience as a car salesman and train us. His routine consisted of coming into the dealership at one o'clock and coming up to every one of us that had less than three months experience in the business. Once he had gone around and shaken all of our hands, he would call us over into the meeting room for our training sessions. Then, once all the new salesmen were in the training room, he would individually ask us if we had sold any cars since the last time we had all met. One by one we would talk about our recent experiences with our customers and discuss why we thought we didn't make a sale or why the customer had bought from us. Pretty standard, right?

After two months of going to this mandatory training session taught by Jerry, it became very boring having to hear the same things over and over. "Make sure you go over the warranty!" he would say. "Always listen to your customer! Make sure they love the car and it meets all their needs before you ask them for the sale!" I was fine with everything Jerry was teaching us because it made sense, but that ended when he started telling us that this business was the only way we could make good money in our lives. He would constantly try to motivate everyone in the room by guaranteeing all of us a manager's position within two years of being in the car business if we could consistently average twenty cars sold every month. As a manager, your average salary was between $120,000-$150,000 depending on the dealership and how many cars are being sold by the salesman. Sure, that's a decent amount of money, but in retrospect that was before taxes. Also, I truly believed that kind of money was considered chump change in the grand scheme of things. I only say that because that wasn't the way I defined and pictured myself being financially free.

Towards the end of the new salesman training, Jerry started asking us one by one if we were excited to become managers. When it came to my turn to say yes, I looked Jerry straight in the eyes and confidently said "No."

(Going back to that lesson of working in silence, this was the perfect place to implement that. I should have just let this go by, but unfortunately my stubbornness got the best of me.)

The puzzled look Jerry gave me was priceless. Almost immediately, his facial expression changed from confused to a subtler "What the fuck?" expression. His poise changed slightly to a defensive position by creating distance between him and I. He leaned back into his chair and crossed his legs to create an almost barrier type of block. Once he was in position, he began to ask why I was in this business in the first place. I replied I had quit my previous job in order to pursue more sales practice. I made it clear that my intentions were to learn as much as I needed to about the car selling business in order to chase my dreams. I wasn't there to invest ten plus years of my life into a career I saw as having a dead end. When Jerry heard what I had to say, he told everyone to take a ten-minute break to kind of clear the tension that had developed inside the training room. Everyone in the room stood up and headed towards the exit at the same time and my mission was to be at the front end of this group solely because I had a feeling Jerry wanted to speak with me.

I was able to get a few steps outside the door before I heard Jerry asking me to stay. I tried acting like I hadn't heard him due to all the noise coming from the loud speaking salesmen, but karma had another thing in mind. A few of the salesmen were calling out to me letting me know that Jerry wanted me to stay and speak with him. Knowing there was no escape from this, I turned around and headed back into the room. When everyone had left and it was only Jerry and I, he asked me to shut the door behind me and sit down. I closed the door and sat down in a chair in front of the big wooden desk Jerry was sitting behind.

Here's where I think Jerry took what I had to say very personal because it was obvious his demeanor had now changed. Raising his voice, Jerry began to say, "What's going with this rebellious attitude you've had lately? Are you even serious about working here? Seriously I'm getting tired of it. Do you really think being some sort of rebel is going to make you any money and get you anywhere in this business? You better start changing your attitude or else you're not going to last long here." His tone of voice made it very clear he was angry. What I thought was going to be a quick conversation, had turned into more of a lecture.

Jerry paused for a few seconds before he optimistically asked again, "Do you want to be a manager?" I assertively, all whilst staying composed, told him my goals were not to become a manager. My goals were to learn as much as I could from the car selling business and apply it to my life as I continued my journey to becoming financially free. He then said, "What do you mean? You can make really good money if you sell enough cars every month. You should focus on becoming a manager so you can make $150,000 a year for the rest of your life. What other job are you even going to come close to pulling those types of numbers? That should be your one and only goal."

Here is the part in the conversation where I should have acknowledged his views as his opinion and just let him talk to me until he was done, but I wasn't going to let him speak to me with that kind of tone. I wanted to defend myself and what I truly believed in a respectful way. I took a deep breath and told him my goal was to become financially free and how I wasn't going to be able to do so if I were to primarily focus on becoming a car sales manager for the rest of my life. "Well how else are you going to become financially free?" he said in a very sarcastic tone. I told him the best way to become financially free was to create multiple streams of income.

(If you don't know what multiple streams of income is [MSI], I'll be going over it later in this book.)

"HA! Why should someone like you be thinking about multiple streams of income? That's not something that is possible at your age. It's impossible. That's something only I can do at my age because I have the money for it. You don't have any money to invest like I do because you haven't been selling cars your whole life like I have. All you should be thinking about is how you can sell more cars and become a sales manager," he said in a manner of disbelief. "There are definitely many ways someone at my age can create multiple streams of income. In fact, currently around the world there any many people, even younger than myself, that have successfully accomplished financial freedom by creating multiple streams of income. They're now millionaires." I said replying to his cynical remark. He then continued by saying, "Okay, then how would you even create multiple streams of income at your age. Prove it."

I didn't want to tell him all the ideas I had at the time, simply because I knew better. I went ahead and chose to go with a simpler one. "One of the best ways is to be a freelance writer and write a book to create passive income..." but before I could finish my sentence, Jerry interrupted me by saying "You're not going make any money writing a book. I know two people that have written a book and haven't made any money on it. Do you even know what it takes to write a book in the first place?" He said. "Yes, I do. I'm currently writing a book right now. In fact, I've been learning how to create passive income from multiple streams by investing in trainings millionaires have offered to the public." He looked at me like I was crazy for what I had just said. "No, No, NO. That's crazy talk. You need to stop living up here in La La Land and forget that crap. Stop chasing those dreams. You need to focus on selling cars," Jerry said.

I was surprised and almost shocked to hear him say that, so I had to ask him to clarify. "So, you're telling me not to follow my dreams and just sell cars the rest of my life?" He followed up my question by saying, "What I'm saying is you shouldn't be thinking about that nonsense right now. These programs you're buying aren't going to make you any money and you won't be able to create multiple streams of income right now in your life anyways. It's impossible. You just can't do it." I then remembered that night at my friend's house and realized that no matter what I said I wasn't going to convince him on my views and no matter what he said it wasn't going to change what I believed to be true. I knew that this was only going to go in circles, so I decided that it just wasn't worth trying to persuade someone who was that cynical. I thought to myself, "I should just agree with him and nod to everything he has to say so I can get out of this office." What happened next was exactly that. I nodded to everything he had to say and acted like I had a change of heart.

  The conversation then ended and I let myself out of the room. I walked back to my desk and sat down to really digest everything that had just happened in that conversation. As I was thinking to myself, one of my coworkers that had left the room earlier with the rest of the group came up to me and asked what had gone on in that room. After I explained everything that happened and reiterated everything Jerry said, my coworker couldn't believe what Jerry had told me. He called out Jerry as being ignorant and closed minded. Shortly after I was done talking to my coworker and was back to being alone at my desk, my attention was directed to my left as I could tell someone was walking towards me. I lifted and turned my head to see that it was Jerry. As he got closer to me he began saying, "You have to make sure your head is in the right place. You can't be off in La La Land while your career as a car salesman suffers. You know, I really do see you being in this business," and that's when I interrupted him and said, "Yes, I was meant to be in business. It just might not be THIS business. You have to keep in mind that what worked for you might not work for me, and you should respect that." Jerry began to shake his head from side to side signifying he wasn't happy to hear what I had to say.

"Do you read?" he asked. "You need to start reading the right books so you open up that mind of yours." I replied by assuring him that I did read books. I told him I read one book per week to make sure I was constantly learning new ways to advance in my journey. Finally, Jerry was done speaking to me and walked away.

A lot of people in your life will not accept the new and better you. Cut off anyone that doesn't support who you're becoming. They are not your true friends. "But what if the people that don't believe in me or support me are my parents, Carlos?" Sometimes you have to do what is necessary to get ahead. Sometimes being around certain negativity and toxicity will hold you back from getting to where you want to go and need to be. If you truly don't want to cut someone out, then just start telling them less. You can still have them in your life, you just don't have to involve them as much on the road to your success. You don't have include them in your plans. Remember that it's imperative you work in silence. And above all, don't feel bad for outgrowing people that had the chance to grow with you.

Close The Gap: Skip The Ladder And Take The Elevator

You must begin to find the right resources of education that will allow you to skip walking up the stairs of success. Knowledge will allow you to surpass the obstacles that have been laid down before you on this path, so make sure the information you receive is reliable.

The next big questions are: "What exactly do I need to study? Where do I find this information? Who's going to teach me?" Most of you reading this book might be thinking that going to school or going back to school would be the best place to find your answers. You are probably thinking this is the best way to walk up the stairs of success because there has always been the premise of "Go to school. Get a job. Work hard. Pay off your debt. Invest in stocks by paying someone to trade them for you and hope they know what they're doing." Unfortunately, there are many problems with that premise. For example, the amount of weight placed on newly graduate shoulders to decide the one thing they will have to stick with and do for the rest of their life is absurd. Do you really think giving that kind of responsibility to someone at the age of eighteen is a good idea? For the person reading this book right now who is over the age of thirty, do you still have the same mentality now than when you were eighteen? No? Didn't think so. There's a big reason why so many young adults end up switching their major halfway through their college journey. Sometimes more than just once, too. If you continue to believe and follow this premise you will be setting yourself up for financial suicide. Following this premise will make you a slave to money for the rest of your life and that's a really scary thing.

What else is scary is the crippling financial bind you get into with student loans. You're told to go to school and get a job, but as you know, the jobs today are not paying enough for you to afford college. So now you have to borrow money from the bank and are left with all this student loan debt. Keep in mind that the job you're working is not going to pay you enough to pay off the loans quickly before interest kicks in. That cycle will continue to get worse and worse the more debt you have and the longer it takes for you to pay it all off. That is a huge problem many fall trap to.

I also find it to be very ironic that the whole reason on why we all go to school is to prepare us for life, yet by the time you were eighteen and graduated high school, did you feel you were remotely equipped and prepared for the important things life had to throw at you? In school we are taught to learn about isosceles triangles and the history of our country, which is great content, but honestly you could wait to learn about that when you're thirty years-old. School is adamant about teaching this type of curriculum to their students to make them "well rounded," yet most people today don't know the basics of investing their money, creating cash-flow, or really understanding how to create appreciating assets that will take care of them throughout the rest of their life. Look, I'm not saying school isn't important. It's vital that people go to school to learn a profession and become a contributing member of society because it's a core component of culture. We need law enforcers, firefighters, soldiers, lawyers, doctors, etc. What I'm saying is we need to understand that just because someone has a college degree and a great profession, it doesn't mean they won't fall into the same trap and suffer financially. In fact, a lot of doctors and lawyers, which are perceived to be well paying professions, actually have more money problems and financial stress than the average blue-collar middle-class worker. How is that possible if some lawyers and doctors are making well over six figures? The problem lies in the thought that more money will solve the problem. For example, because a lot of doctors are paid more than the average middle-class worker, they're able to afford a more expensive house, car, boat, and lifestyle. Which means their bills are a lot higher because of it. That's why you see a lot of doctors and lawyers having big financial problems.

So, what do they do in order to continue supporting their families and continue enjoying their luxuries? The doctor will raise his fees in order to increase the amount of his income. By doing so, it creates a domino effect. When the doctor raises his fees, health care becomes more expensive. When health care becomes more expensive, fast food establishment employees want a raise. When fast food establishment employees receive a raise, school teachers want a raise, too. When school teachers get their raise, it raises all of our taxes and prices go up. So, on and so forth. Eventually, the gap between those that are able to afford it (The wealthy), and those who won't be able to (lower and middle class), will be so wide that chaos will break out. Sadly, every day our country continues down this path by increasing the gap. History has shown us that great civilizations have always been able to bounce back from any foreign attack but have never been able to rise again by ultimately being destroyed and falling from within. Unfortunately, we're only taught to memorize historical dates in school, and not the lesson.

    For people living a paycheck to paycheck life, the thought of not being able to pay your bills on time can be very stressful and concerning. They think, "If I work a little harder at the office this quarter, I'm sure I'll be promoted and get the raise I've been wanting!" Or, "I wish I was making more money so I could take some time off work and spend more time with my friends and family." The idea that more money will solve your financial issues is an illusion. As we've already discussed, that won't solve the problem. The real problem resides within the education system itself. What's wrong with it is that it's flawed and has failed us in many ways. I'm not saying it's the teachers that are causing our children to fail, I'm saying it's the school system itself. It's obsolete. Think about it. School is not build for entrepreneurs, it's build for workers because you're taught to play within the lines. The educational system is failing entrepreneurs every single day because of the way it's been structured to create employees and not business owners. There's nothing being taught about opening your own business or mapping your way into the entrepreneurial market. You may be asking, "But what about going to school for business and marketing, Carlos?" Well, there are two problems with taking that route. See if you can find them in this simplified scenario.

Imagine you're eighteen years-old again and are thinking about attending college. You don't really know what to do with your life, but you're positive you want to be making "good money." After a little bit of researching which professions have high grossing incomes on Google, you decide you want to major in business and apply to a couple universities of your choice. You begin submitting an application for each college and end up waiting a couple of weeks, maybe months to hear back from each institution. Finally, you begin to receive letters and emails from each college either rejecting you or accepting you. After being accepted to most of your options, you receive a letter in the mail informing you that you have been accepted into the college of your dreams! Congratulations!

Before you know it, it's move-in day. You load up your car with all your bags, crates, and boxes that are carrying all the essentials you believe you'll need your first semester. Once you arrive to your dorm or place of housing, you start to unload everything off the car and begin to move it all into your room. You thank Mom or Dad for their best wishes this semester and hug them goodbye. Shortly after they leave, you realize that this is the first time you'll be testing your independence and the reality of the commitment to this college begins to settle in.

A light turns on over your head as you remember your first day of class is next week and you still haven't purchased any of the textbooks you'll be needing in class. You eventually decide to go to the school's library to buy them. When you're finally at the cashier, your stomach begins to sink as the total price of the sale continues to duplicate with each book passing through the scanner. You then pay the whopping price for your four textbooks and hope they will be worth the money you just paid, but honestly you know deep down you'll mostly be using it as a coaster for your coffee.

Welcome to your first day of class. The professor comes into the room and introduces himself. As he shares some personal information about himself, he encourages everyone else attending his class to share a bit about themselves in order to break the ice. Beginning from one end of the room and ending on the opposite side, one by one each student stands up to share some information about themselves and why they have decided to take this particular class. When it's finally your turn to speak, you decide to talk about where you're from, what sport you played in high school, and the reason you chose to attend this class. You declare you've chosen to major in business because someday you hope to become a self-employed millionaire. You hear a few chuckles coming from your classmates, as well as receive some odd stares before you sit back down and hear the professor add, "Don't we all..."

As the professor tells the class to open up their textbooks and turn to page fifteen, you hear someone from the front row volunteer to pass out the itinerary for the semester. When the sheet of paper is finally in front of you, you notice the itinerary has laid out your curriculum in chronological order. The bullet point list begins with "Origins of business in America," and is followed by "What are the biggest corporations today, How teamwork makes the dream work, The power of networking," and so on. After reading these topics, a puzzled expression consumes your face as you think to yourself that there wasn't anything mentioned about creating your own business, learning how to manage and multiply your own money, or even the importance of learning how to invest. You remind yourself not to be cynical and be optimistic about this course and follow it through to the end. I mean, it did cost you or your family a lot of money to be there in the first place. Not to mention those coasters! I mean textbooks...

As time begins to fly by and you find yourself months into this course, you start to question the curriculum being taught in class. You've even noticed a lot of the context provided by these expensive textbooks have been outdated for quite some time now. The end of class nears and you have decided to stay afterwards in order to ask the professor some questions. As the classroom begins to empty, you make your way to the front of the room. "Hey professor, do you have a moment to speak?" "Sure. What can I do for you?" he says. "Well, we're a couple months into class and I was just wondering if we're going to talk about how to start our own businesses and possibly how to invest." You ask in a hopeful manner. "Unfortunately, that's not part of the curriculum. I don't think that's something you'll be going over in some of your other classes either." he says confused. "Why do you ask?" "Well, I thought we were going to learn how to create our own businesses and learn how to invest so we could create passive income. I've been doing some research and turns out a lot of the stuff being taught out of the textbooks is outdated. Especially now that almost all of the marketing done by businesses is done on social media. I've also been reading some books millionaires have published and they almost all commonly say not to do what our textbooks say we should do."

"If you don't think what I've been teaching for twenty years is in anyway constructive, why are you taking my course in the first place?" the professor says in a different demeanor now. "I'm not questioning you as a professor, I'm just trying to understand why we're not learning how to become entrepreneurs so we can one day become financially free."

"There are many ways you can become financially free through business. You could one day possibly become one of the top guys in a company and make the big bucks." Your professor says in a confident tone. "Sure, but the problem there would still be me having to work for someone else. I don't want to have a boss the rest of my life. I want to be able to wake up whenever I want. I want to spend my time however I wish. I want to wake up every morning with more money in my bank account than I had the previous day. Like I said, I don't want to have a boss for the rest of my life."

"Well you're always going to pretty much has a boss. I've always had boss throughout my teaching career." Your professor says.

"So, you've never been a millionaire?" you ask almost skeptical. "No, but I've met a lot of them and have worked with them too."

Were you able to spot the problems? For starters, a lot of what is being taught in school today has become obsolete. Technology is continuously changing and evolving every single day making it harder to keep track off. Because technology is continuously changing, by the time the author of a textbook finishes writing it, publishing it, has it stocked and sold in schools, and is finally being taught by professors, more than a year would have already passed since the textbook's inception. We live in a day and age where it's important to continuously adapt to current business marketing strategies and trends in order to stay relevant. If you're business is not up to date, it will suffer because of it and be left behind.

The second issue I personally have a problem with was the fact that we go to school in order to learn from our professors who in turn never truly had much real-world experience with what they're teaching. Just like my scenario above, I too had a similar experience. The fact that I wasn't being taught how to create my own business, invest/manage my own money, or learn how to create passive income by someone ironically teaching a business course with moderate to little experience outside the classroom was almost insulting. Unfortunately for me, it was a bit late to get a refund for the class seeing as how it had been a couple of months since the start of the semester.

"Okay. If going to school is not the best or most efficient way to become financially free, where do I go to learn?" I hear you and honestly this question isn't as hard to answer as you might think it is. The answer is something I'm sure you've heard numerous times, but for a good reason. Knowing what to study, what not to study, who to listen to and who not to listen to is very nerve racking due to the fact that you've never done this before. How do you know what you're doing has you on the right path? How do you know you're not wasting your time? Where do you go to ensure that?

Take a quick moment to digest what I'm about to tell you. On average, about 100,000 people move into and out of Los Angeles (L.A.) every year. Those that move into L.A. go there in order to pursue their dreams. Dreams of becoming A-list movie stars, famous artists, rappers, music producers, etc. Some of them accomplish their goals, yet most of them don't quite make it and find themselves moving out L.A. within a couple years. Why do you think that is? Why do some make it and most don't? What sets those who make it apart than the vast majority that never do?

Lucky for you I've already figured that out. Here's a hint. Jay-Z the rapper had one. Bill Gates had one. Ellen DeGeneres had one. Warren Buffett had one. Oprah even had two! Do you know what it is I'm talking about yet? It's Mentors.

The answer may be simple, but where do you even find a mentor? For most of you, a mentor means you'll need to go out and find someone who is already successful in the field you want to become successful in. In which case you'll need to find out exactly how to get ahold of them in order to introduce yourself in person and ask them for their help. This may be easy in some cases, but a lot of the time it won't be. Most successful businessmen, entrepreneurs, and moguls won't allow just anyone to come into their inner circle and let you to ask for their help as they are tired of people reaching out to them just to ask for free handouts. That reason alone will make it very hard to be taken under someone else's wing.

Let's say you somehow are able to find a mentor with a lot of success and experience in a certain niche. If you're able to convince them to mentor you, you'd be able to close the knowledge gap. What do I mean by "The knowledge

Gap?" Imagine you are twenty-one years-old and you've decided to find a mentor. After a couple of days of searching and researching on Google, you've chosen a highly successful real estate agent to be the person you contact. The next day you call his office and set up an appointment to meet with this guru. When you arrive, you are invited into his office where you meet him and introduce yourself. After a while of explaining to him the reason behind why you are there, you finally tell him that you will work for him for free if he is willing to show you everything he knows and has learned over the course of his forty-year career in real estate. After a moment of silence, he smiles at you and gladly accepts your proposition. It then takes you about two solid years to really retain everything he's learned over the course of forty years in real estate. Because of that, you didn't have to spend forty years of your life learning the exact same things the guru did and be where he is forty years from now. Instead, you've learned forty years' worth of real estate knowledge in only two years. You can now continue where he left off, and what's amazing is you're still only twenty-three years-old. That's what I mean by closing the knowledge gap.

Mentors are great, but not all are easily accessible. Like I've already mentioned, some of them are extremely hard to get ahold of and most of the greatest minds to ever walk this planet are dead. But what if I told you there was a way you could be mentored by every great mind to ever walk this Earth. Alive and dead. Would you believe me? It's true. In fact, a lot of them are in my room right now. I'm of course talking about books. It is because of books that we are able to learn everything a great mentor has to offer. Think about it. If you aren't able to have Elon Musk personally mentor you from your home or his, you are still able to receive the same message through his books. The same idea goes for anyone successful in history. In fact, the very first mentor I ever had gave me one of the best pieces of advice that I will reiterate for the rest of my life. We were neighbors at the time so it was easy for me to just walk out the front door of my house and head next door. He had invited me over to help him with some bricking because he was planning on placing it around his house. He didn't have to do that, but I told him I wanted to learn bricking because I had never done it before and was interested in learning.

My house was one of only two houses in the entire neighborhood that had towering pine trees on its property, so I wanted to be able to lay some brick around them and make them look a lot more appealing. A couple of hours into it, I was very impressed with the way he was laying brick and decided to ask him who had taught him. The next thing he said was one of the best pieces of advice I could have ever been given. He told me no one had taught him how to do it and then said, "If you ever want to learn how to do something just pick up a book and read it." I thought to myself, "I mean I guess, but the thing is I don't like to read." In fact, I actually thought that reading books was a waste of time. I also didn't enjoy reading because It hurt my eyes and head to do so. But I thought about what he had to say about books and kept that advice with me.

Fast forward to high school. It wasn't until sophomore year that I was assigned to read the book *Fahrenheit 451* by Ray Bradbury that my whole perspective on reading changed. Reading that book taught me the value and importance of literature in society and how it was vital to our personal growth. After that I started to view books differently. I saw them to be more of an eye-opener than anything else. Although my view on books had changed I still wasn't reading as much as I should have. It wasn't until later in life when I turned twenty years-old and was really struggling financially, that I came across the quote "The more you learn, the more you earn" by Warren Buffett, and I truly began closing the knowledge gap. I started reading books about topics I was interested in and curious about. I realized how crucial it was to read books and how much they contributed in correlation to one's own success. I've made it a routine of mine to read one to two books per week believe it or not. I'm not saying I immediately started to read every book I could get a hold of. I had to build up to it. For those of you that don't read that much per week or at all, nothing's impossible! I started reading five pages per day and within weeks I was reading fifty pages per day! I promise you'll get better if you make it a daily routine. Not only will you progressively get better at reading, your knowledge will begin to expand. Why do you think CEOs on average read fifty-two books per year? That's because they understand that they don't know everything and must continue learning in order to become more successful.

    You have to view each book as a treasure chest. Inside every single book is a hidden golden nugget of wisdom or advice that can be revolutionary if applied correctly to your life. But be careful not to read the wrong books. Just like advice, there's a lot of it out there, but not all are remotely helpful. Remember, "One cannot collect all the beautiful shells on the beach. One can collect only a few, and they are more beautiful because of it."

I'm a very strong believer that through books and mentors you will find your way to success. It is in our ability to learn from others mistakes and win's that will allow you to surpass the majority. Think about why is it that we sometimes feel lost in life? Simply, it's because we don't have someone there guiding us.

Why The Rich Get Richer And Poor Get Poorer

Why does it seem like the rich keep getting richer? How is it that the more we get paid, the poorer we become? Well, what if I told you the reason the rich get wealthier is because they're more focused on their education than their money? It's true. We've already discussed the dangers of thinking more money solves the problem, so I thought it'd be important to discuss and understand what really solves the problem of being poor. If more money doesn't solve the problem then what does? Your intelligence is what will solve your problems and produce more money. The more financially literate you become, the better chance you'll have at acquiring more wealth. I say this because what truly makes someone rich isn't the amount of money they make, it's the amount of money they keep. What do I mean by that? In order to answer that question, we must look this through a different perspective.

Every single day thousands of people go to the gas station to purchase a lottery ticket in hopes of getting lucky and winning millions of dollars. Eventually, someone will be lucky enough to purchase the right ticket and win the jackpot. There's a big ceremony to give the lucky winner their prize money and congratulate them, but what happens next? Statistics show that almost all lottery winners go back to being poor and working for their money again within a few years. Why do you think that is? The answer is simply because they spend all of their money on liabilities that in return don't make any more money for them. Instead of investing in their future, they make the mistake of buying luxuries first. You see this happening primarily with professional athletes. After years of being paid millions and millions of dollars for their talents and skills, eventually they get too old to play anymore. When players retire, we sometimes never expect them to end up working at a company again making minimum wage. This sounds strange, but it does happen. After professional players retire, if they aren't mentored or consulted on investing in assets, they usually are not able to keep up with their expenses and have to file for bankruptcy.

  Imagine how strange it would be to enter your favorite fast food establishment and have a retired pro-athlete that was once making millions of dollars per year take your order? It sounds like it would be a cool opportunity to be able to meet them, but I'm sure you would feel some sort of pity knowing the situation they're in. So, what do you do in order to avoid falling into the trap some retired pro-athletes and many lottery winners find themselves in? You need to invest in assets. How do you do that? By understanding the difference between an asset and a liability. One of the biggest reasons why people are wealthy is because they have already learned the difference between liabilities and assets. They've also learned that being rich and wealthy are two different things. Let's say you quit your job today. Your wealth is defined by how many days forward you will be able to survive before spending all your money.

Why do you think the top 1% of the population earns and controls 96% of all the money? Do you think that happened by accident? No, they've harnessed the power of assets in order to raise their wealth. A lot of the time the poor and the middle-class acquire liabilities thinking they're assets. It's important you pay attention to what I am about to teach you. You want to make sure your cash-flow is that of a wealthy person and you discontinue the habits of a poor person. You can do that by simply copying what it is wealthy people do.

One of the great things I learned being a car salesman was more people were inclined to buy the car when they better understood the warranty. I realized most people are visual learners so I began to draw out the warranty in front of them using a notebook. In order to make sure you understand the difference between an asset and a liability, I will be creating diagrams for all you visual learners out there.

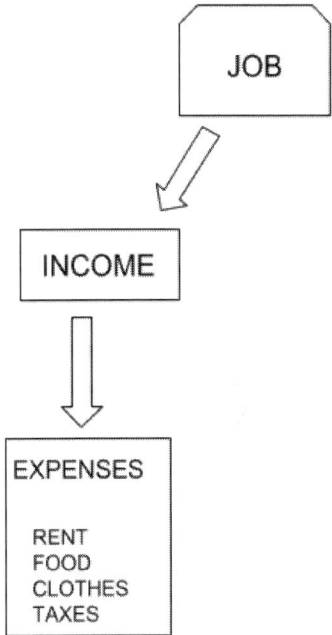

: This right here is the visual representation of the cash-flow of a poor person. This person is currently living a paycheck to paycheck life and barely surviving. Their only source of income is coming from their job. They only have enough money to pay for their rent, food, clothes and taxes. Because they are poor, they won't have a car so they'll have to either walk, ride their bike or pay for public transportation.

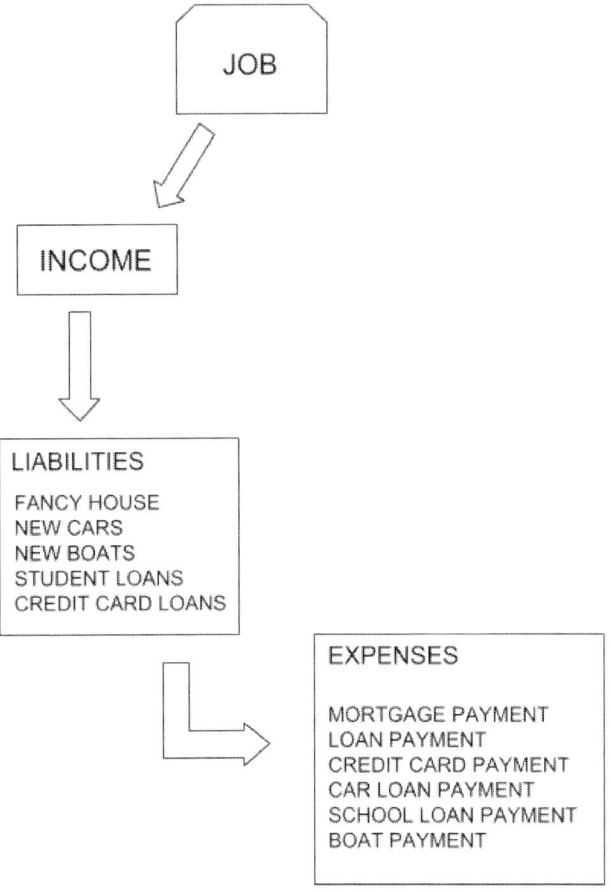

: This right here is the visual representation of the cash-flow of a middle-class person. Although this person is making more money at his/her job and are able to afford more luxuries, they still fall into the trap of living a paycheck to paycheck life because they lack assets. All the money these people earn from their job gets spent on liabilities.

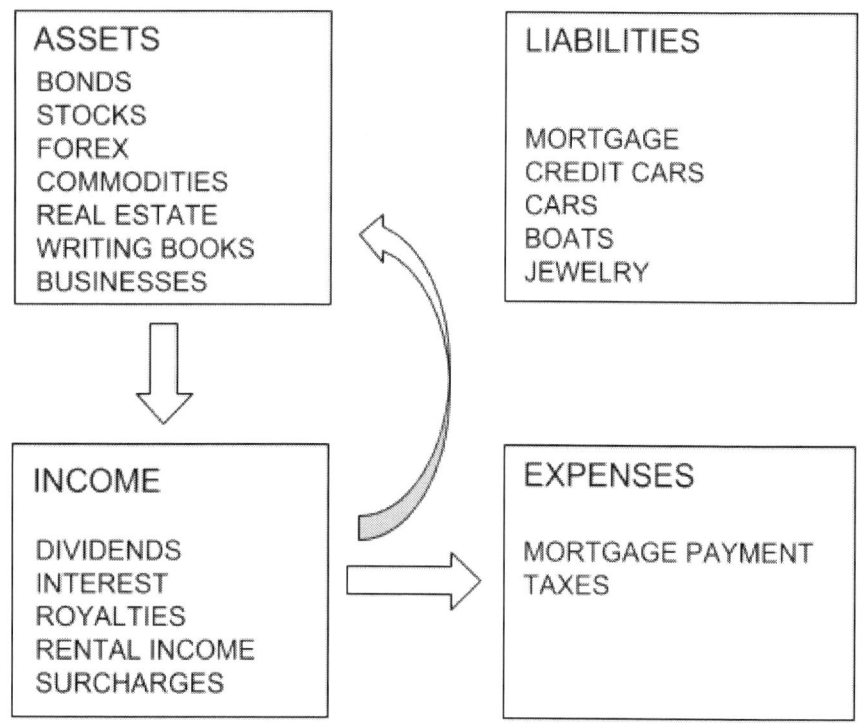

: This right here is the visual representation of the cash-flow of a wealthy person. Notice that their income comes from the assets they have acquired over the years. Wealthy people invest in buying and owning assets and are only able to purchase luxuries if their assets yield enough return on their investment (ROI). If their assets do not produce enough income to purchase a luxury, wealthy people will invest in more assets to create more passive income until they are able to afford it.

Keep in mind these diagrams are oversimplified in order to better understand cash-flow. It's obvious that everyone has living expenses including food, clothes, clean water, and shelter. Now that you have studied these visuals, it'll be easier to understand why assets are important to grow your wealth. Now, be careful not to mistake a liability for an asset. Assets put money in your pocket whether you work or not, which then yields passive income. There was a time not too long ago that many people believed their house was an asset. Unfortunately, many people were proved wrong due to the banks and market crashing in 2008. "If our houses aren't assets then why do our banks tell us they are?"

Well, you're absolutely right. The banks weren't lying when they told you the house you were purchasing or currently owned was an asset. What they didn't clarify was that it was an asset for the bank! When banks lend you money to purchase a home, they are able to make more money than they initially lent you through interest. Simply put, that's their asset. In fact, a house is actually a liability. Having to continuously put money into fixing it up and maintaining your home could sometimes result in losing additional capital that could have been invested into creating an asset. That extra capital could have also been invested towards an already existing asset causing it to grow.

I'm not saying you shouldn't buy a house. In fact, I think it's very important to buy and payoff your home. What I'm trying to help you understand is the difference between an asset and a liability. Many people that don't understand the difference between the two and sometimes end up buying a very expensive house expecting it to raise in value. Sadly, many of those houses today have yet to raise in value and have only gone down in value.

Liabilities are not the way to go. You must find a way to acquire assets or create assets. It's also not likely to become wealthy off just one asset. Sure, there have been certain occasions where someone has created a product that has sold like crazy and yielded them millions, but those are the outliers. The idea that one thing will make you wealthy isn't always the best one to have. This goes hand-in-hand with someone asking a millionaire what's the one way they too can become millionaires. The thing is there is no "one way" to become wealthy. You must create multiple streams of income in order to become wealthy. Eventually, all those streams will amount to millions!

Think about what I'm about to ask you. If you were to get fired from your job right now, where else would you receive income from? You see, most people only have one source of income and I cannot stress how financially dangerous that is. If you put all your eggs in one basket and you drop that basket, all of your eggs are bound to break. Same goes for your income. If you depend on only one source of income, what will happen when you lose it?

I once asked the same question to one of my coworkers and it blew their mind to say the least. She told me she had never thought about it that way, and how much it scared her to think of the idea of her losing everything and having to move back in with her parents at age 32. She asked me what she could do to prevent "all her eggs from breaking," and I told her it was important she acquire or create multiple streams of income through assets.

Another reason middle-class people struggle with money is because they are driven by greed. Many people desire a new car, new clothes, a better handbag, or that new fancy watch, so the first thing they do when they get paid is go out and purchase these luxuries. That is the perfect recipe for staying poor the rest of your life. What wealthy people understand is that before they're able to purchase something they desire, they have to make sure their assets produce enough income for it. If not, they acquire more assets to increase their income. Do you understand? Again, poor people buy luxuries first. Wealthy people buy luxuries last.

"The what should I invest in for my future? Should I participate in the 401(k)-plan my job is offering me?" Well, here's the thing. More and more employees are investing into a 401(k)-plan thinking they are preparing themselves for their future. Employees who participate in these plans assume responsibility for their retirement income by contributing part of their salary into this plan. However, hidden fees in retirement plans are a major problem for people planning their retirement. When the 401(k) was first created in 1984, it gave employees the opportunity to build wealth by making a tax-deductible monthly subscription to a retirement account straight from their paychecks. This was a great idea seeing as how you could definitely erect a mountain of wealth by simply saving a very small portion of your paycheck. Slowly, every month your mound of riches increased with each contribution. Now, over 90 million Americans participate in a 401(k)-plan. Combined that's more than SIX TRILLION dollars ($6,000,000,000,000) currently invested in these 401(k)'s. That alone has made it America's greatest investment for future financial security.

But, eventually that security became a flimsy concept. Because there was so much money being stored in that pot, financial firms found it hard not to stick their hands into it. It wasn't until recently in 2012 that the government finally forced financial firms to produce detailed disclosures of how much money they were charging their customers 401(k) savings account. Believe it or not, for almost three decades, the companies that were offering 401(k)-plans were not required by law to disclose how much they were charging their customers. This was where many hidden fees began to arise. Unfortunately, even with laws being implemented, firms are still taking advantage of their customers. The whole system has been able to dodge legal implications by creating thirty to fifty-page documents disclosing sub-charges and additional fees for their services. Unless you're a lawyer or have a degree in finance you probably won't understand all that jargon companies print on those disclosures. It's sad to admit that most employees sign these disclosures trusting their employers won't take advantage of them.

In fact, did you know that 71% of employees enrolled in some sort of 401(k)-plan don't even know there are hidden fees. That's right! 92% of employees also admit to not knowing what these hidden fees are! Not only are you being charged fees by the mutual funds in your 401(k)-plan, but you're also being charged additional fees by the plan provider administering your 401(k)-plan. Here's just a short list of the many categories of expenses and charges these companies have invented: bookkeeping expenses, trustee expenses, transactional expenses, administrative expenses, communication expenses, investment expenses, legal expenses.

So, what all these expenses and charges costing you? Well, if you're someone making $30,000 per year and are saving 5% of your income, over the time of your working life these fees would cost you $154,794. Think about that for just a minute. That is more than five years of income combined being taken away from an employee without realizing it's happening. It gets worse for those making more than $30,000 a year. For someone making $90,000 a year, you would end up losing $277,000 in fees. This is why you must be aware of how the financial market will try to make it harder for you to invest your money into a 401(k)-plan. The best form of defense against these firms is to educate yourself. To learn more about the best ways to protect yourself against these firms, I encourage you to read *Unshakable* by Tony Robbins.

"Well, all this talk about investing into the wrong place and being charged hidden fees scares me. I fear I'll lose my money or get most of it taken away. So, I'd honestly rather just save my money in a personal savings account." Typically, this is the next thought of someone once they've learned about the hidden fees. If you save your money, save to invest. Don't just save your money and have it sit there in an account. The average APY (annual percentage yield, or interest) of a savings account is only 0.06%. If you had a single dollar in that savings account, every year you'd be gaining six cents in interest. That's not a whole lot. Yes, there are some saving accounts out there that offer closer to 1%, but the truth is your money will never grow as fast as you need it to. You'd be better off using what's known as "The Latte Factor." To sum up what this is, the "Latte Factor" refers to the tiny expenditures that you make each day without thinking about them. Thus, the name itself refers to the daily purchase of a latte or coffee. Have you ever thought about how much a $5.00 coffee is really costing you? Here's a scenario of how most people participate in the latte factor.

You start off each day with a latte and a bagel, costing you about $5.00. Later, being at work you decide to use the vending machine which will cost you about $2.00 a visit. On your way home, you often crave some sort of snack and decide to buy it costing you another $3.00. Keep in mind you also go out to eat about two days a week and average $10.00 spent per meal. Little expenditures, right? In a single seven-day week, that added up to $80.00. After a year of accumulation, the total comes out to be $4,160. If you were to invest that amount each year at 10% annual return until you were 65 years-old, that total would come out to $1.92 million dollars. In other words, that morning coffee and those occasional meals are stopping you from becoming a millionaire. If you're between the ages of 18 and 30 and are interested in learning more about how to become a millionaire with little to no effort by the time you retire, I encourage you to read the *Automatic Millionaire* by David Bach.

All this can be very intimidating, I know, but it's important you learn about this so you don't lose all your money on your journey to becoming financially free. Always be mindful of what you are going to invest in or your run the high risk of losing your money. Just like Warren Buffett says, "Risk comes from not knowing what you are doing." There are a lot of books and training programs out on the market that will help you better understand different forms of investing. For those of you that don't want to spend their money right from the get, I suggest using video sharing platforms such as YouTube to watch free videos on any asset topic you're curious about. However, I don't always recommend using what's free seeing as how you usually get what you paid for.

Now that you're aware of the differences between habits the poor and the wealthy people make, it's your responsibility to apply them to your life. Remember to study the cash-flow charts I've provided for you in the last couple of pages. Make sure you understand why the wealthy get wealthier and the poor get poorer. Once more to really drive the point home: Poor people will constantly purchase luxuries first which will in turn create financial problems. Wealthy people invest in assets first and purchase luxuries last.

Experiments Equal Success

As you've seen on popular social media apps, there are so many people promoting ways to make money. From online drop shipping stores to trading currencies and stocks. But there's a big problem with this. In fact, it's one of the main reasons most people never make any money in the first place. Know what the problem is? The problem is so many people are out here trying to chase down the money. People come across promoted videos on social media about ways others have accumulated their fortune and how you could too by simply signing up for their online course. I'm not here to discredit anyone's online course, I'm here to identify another reason why you're having trouble acquiring mass wealth. Like I said, you're chasing the money. Want to know how to really make money? Solve problems. "What? Like math?" No silly, I'm talking about finding a solution to problems everyday people have. For example, why did you buy this book?

You have to stop thinking about chasing money and start focusing on solving the many problems many people encounter every day. Okay, let's say you stop chasing money and start paying very close attention to your daily routine to try and identify any particular issues you might have that could be solved. Eventually you come across one that you think you can solve! Okay so now what? How do you go about it? Easy: **Experiment.**

Yup. Experiment. Let me put things into perspective. You're about to go on your first date with someone you've matched on Tinder. You've never met the other person before this night, but you two seem to hit it off in a great way. You start to think half way through the night, "Man this date's been going really well. I hope it keeps going the way it has been so far, but if it turns out to be a bust at least I got a free meal out of it." (I'm looking at you, ladies) The end of the night now approaches. Right before the date ends, your Tinder date says, "You know what? I thought this date went pretty well and you're crazy beautiful," as he goes down on one knee. He then pulls out a ring out of his right-hand pocket and proceeds to ask you to marry them. "WHAT THE HELL?" is right.

You wouldn't marry someone after the first date, right? That's just ridiculous. Sadly, a lot of you reading this are guilty of jumping into a serious commitment with a business after the "first date." Here's what I mean. Let's say your dream is to open a coffee shop in the middle of your town. You find a place to lease in the center of a plaza and decide to put a whopping $50,000 as a down payment with a monthly payment of $10,000. At first you take a couple days to think it over. You ask for the opinion of some of your closest friends to see if it'd be a good idea. Although very few of them tell you that it wouldn't be worth it, most of them tell you to go for it because it would be cool if their good friend was the owner of a coffee shop. Some of them even reference getting free coffee in the future. After days of thinking it over and getting input from your friends and family, you remember you know someone that has opened a coffee shop before. It's been awhile since you've last spoken to him, but you believe his guidance on this would be important enough to consider asking for it. You get in contact with the coffee shop owner and tell him your situation. After you finish explaining to him your situation, you ask him for his advice. He looks at you for a moment and says, "You want to spend $50,000 of your own money and open up a coffee shop when you have ZERO experience in this industry. And you expect it to be a success?" Again, why the hell would you marry someone after the first date? Why would you get into a serious commitment with a business you have zero experience in? What you need to do is EXPERIMENT. Here's how you can experiment to see if a coffee selling business would take off in your area with using no more than $100.00 USD.

You decide to create a coffee delivery business out of your kitchen as your first experiment. What you plan on doing is buying your coffee beans wholesale, then go to ten offices where you know people are drinking coffee. You then offer them a free sample of your coffee and ask them to purchase a monthly subscription of $10.00 if they thought the coffee tasted great. You explain to them that every month someone will hand deliver them a pound of your coffee straight to their office. You also tell them that they are able to cancel their subscription whenever they want. After you've established your ten customers, you then hire someone to deliver the coffee and start their pay at $10.00 per hour. You've already tracked the distance between all the offices and know the route shouldn't take longer than fifty minutes to complete. Okay let's now look at this experiment with a bird's eye view:

Buying a pound of coffee for wholesale costs about $6.00. $6.00 of coffee x 10 offices = $60.00 USD spent + $10.00 employment = $70.00 spent. Each office pays you $10.00 to start their subscription which amounts to $100.00. After spending the $70.00, you are left with a PROFIT of $30.00!!! You were able to run an experiment, spend about $70.00, and still make a profit of $30.00 at the end of your first month. If your business takes off just imagine the possibility of success and the continuing profit every month?

Everything you desire in life is possible if you strategize the right way. The only way to know if your business idea will work is to experiment on a small scale. Don't fall into a bind by committing yourself to one business you know nothing about for the rest of your life. Start to experiment every idea you have. A mentor of mine once told me that if he were to run 10 experiments and 8 of them failed, he would actually be happy! Why? Because now he knows which experiments work and which of them didn't make him any money. By paying attention to the results of each experiment, he can now focus on the two experiments that were very successful. The practice of experimenting goes a long way. Most don't understand that the people who are most successful in life are the ones that experiment the most.

The Twelve Decrees Of Money

In order architect your successful future, you must first focus on creating a strong foundation. Follow these rules and apply them to your life and you will know the sweet taste of the fruit of freedom.

Pay Yourself First.

A big problem with accumulating wealth is we tend to think of ourselves last. We prioritize paying our banks, landlords, and bills instead of prioritizing paying ourselves. In other words, the moment we receive our paychecks, we begin to pay everyone else first, and are left to keep and spend whatever is left of our paycheck. Doing this has crippled every chance you have of getting out of the Rat Race because the financial foundation on which you stand is not stable. Fortify your foundation against financial stress by beginning to save no less than one tenth of your earnings every time you are paid. Before you pay anyone else, take out one tenth of your paycheck and begin to save it. If you start to save one tenth every time you are paid, eventually your savings will accumulate to a large sum of money. In due time, your savings will accumulate large enough to find yourself in an emotional state of security and happiness. If you are able to pay yourself more than one tenth, feel free to do so, but remember no less. This sum of wealth must not be touched unless you are planning on using it to create more wealth or using it for that rainy day. If you find yourself not having enough money to pay your bills after saving that one tenth, do not reach into your savings. This should force you to find a way to multiply your earnings in order to pay what you owe. This will teach you the magic of creating wealth.

2. Spend Your Money Only On Necessities.

Be wise enough not to let your emotional desire dictate your expenditures. Spend your money only of the necessities you and your family need. Do not fall into the trap poor people find themselves in. The reason poor people stay poor is because they let their desire for materialistic liabilities take over. The problem with purchasing liabilities is they will not return much, if any, money back to you and will instead require more money to continue using it. For example, purchasing a car will require additional funds to maintain and keep it running well on the road. Remember, the wealthy do not spend their money on luxuries first, they buy them last. Before they are able to purchase a luxury, they make sure their assets are producing enough revenue to buy it. If the assets do not provide enough money at that time, they invest in acquiring more assets until there is enough profit to purchase their luxury.

3. Make Money Your Slave

Once you are willing to fight the urge of buying luxuries first, you must learn to multiply your money. If you continue to be a slave to money, you'll never have a chance at becoming financially free. The problem is most of society is a slave to money and isn't even conscious of it. Because of that, most of the world participates in what's known as the "Rat Race." The rat race is a way of life in which people are caught up in a fiercely competitive struggle for wealth or power. Your goal should be to get out of the Rat Race as soon as possible. The only way to do so is to learn how to make money work for you, instead of you working for it. You need to rewire your thought process of thinking that there is only one way of making money. There are actually endless ways of multiplying your wealth and having it work for you. Your responsibility is to find ways and figure out how to multiply it. The best way to look at it is to imagine that every dollar bill in your account is an employee or yours. The job of each employee is to go out into the world and bring back more employees to work for you. Once the first wave of employees returns with a second generation of employees, repeat the process by sending the first and second wave out into the world in order to have them bring back a third generation of employees. Once you learn to view each dollar as an employee, you'll never have to work for money again.

    There's a true story I'd like to share with you about a high school student named Johnny. Johnny was able to learn how to make money work for him, instead of having him work for it. The year was 2013, and the young man's seventeenth birthday was approaching next month. The one thing he wanted most for his birthday was to have his own car. Out of all his friends, Johnny was the only one that had to ask his parents' permission to borrow the car. He was getting tired of it. It really bothered Johnny when he needed to borrow the car but couldn't because his father was using it.

A week before his birthday, Johnny asked his dad if it would be possible to receive a car as a gift. Johnny was comfortable asking him for a car because his dad was a self-employed businessman making a six figure of annual income. He knew his dad would be able to afford buying him the car.

His dad gave him a strange look and told him he'd think about it. Johnny tried to further convince his dad by bringing up valid points as to why it was important he own his own car, but again his dad just told him he'd think about it.

A week had gone by and it was finally the morning of Johnny's birthday. His dad opened the door to his room and turned on the light. With a great big smile, Johnny's dad said happy birthday to his son and then sat at the foot of his bed. It appeared his father was thinking of something to say next, so Johnny just patiently sat in his bed until his father spoke. "I know you wanted a car for your birthday and every reason you gave me on why you should own one was valid. I cannot argue any of them. The only thing is, I thought I'd take this opportunity to teach you something important. I want to ask something of you." Johnny's dad said.

Johnny looked at his father a bit lost but proceeded to nod his head up and down indicating he was paying attention. "I've decided instead of buying you a car, I'm actually going to give you two thousand dollars. Now, you can decide to either buy yourself an older used car with that money or figure out a way to multiply it and buy yourself a new car. But just know that this is all you will be getting from me for the next year." With that said, Johnny's dad took out the money from his pocket and handed it to him.

Johnny thanked his dad for the birthday wishes and the wonderful gift he had given him. He then got dressed, took his bike out of the garage, and rode straight to the used car dealership fifteen minutes away from his home. When he arrived, Johnny began to walk around the used car lot to see if any car caught his attention. After an hour of walking the lot and being helped by a sale associate, it came down to two vehicle options. His first option had an out the door price of $1,500, and the second option was exactly $2,000 out the door. Johnny really liked his second option but felt like something was holding him back from purchasing the car. The words his father had said to him kept replaying in his mind. Although he really wanted to buy the more expensive car, he also didn't want to spend every dollar his father had given him. After weighing his options, Johnny thought it would be wiser for him to go with the first option instead of the more expensive one. Johnny informed the salesman of his decision and was escorted inside to begin paperwork. Within two hours, Johnny was driving off the parking lot with his newly purchased car.

  As he drove with the windows down letting the wind flow through his hair, the feeling of freedom started to overwhelm him. Johnny finally felt free. As he approached the entrance to his neighborhood, a loud popping noise blasted from the front of the car. All of a sudden smoke began to escape the gaps of the front hood. Johnny was shocked and didn't understand what was happening with the car. He repeatedly pressed on the accelerator, but nothing was happening.

  Eventually the car came to a complete stop on the side of the road. He just couldn't believe what was happening. Johnny got out of his car, lifted the front hood, and witnessed all the smoke coming from the engine. Just by looking at the engine he could tell the car was a goner.

With no way of getting home, his only option was to call his dad and tell him what had happened. When his dad answered and asked how buying the car went, Johnny told his dad about buying the less expensive car and what had happened on the way home from the dealership. After hearing the story, he told Johnny to stay where he was while he drove there to pick him up. Johnny said "Okay. I'll be here." in sad tone before hanging up. He was devastated. This was the first car he had ever bought and the engine had already exploded within being minutes of being in his possession. When his father arrived, he called a tow truck to have the car moved and then gave his son a ride back home. Johnny wasn't in the mood to talk so he was silent the rest of the way home. Later that night Johnny thought about the decision he had made at the dealership earlier and how things probably would have worked out a lot better if he had just bought the more expensive car. Unfortunately, there was nothing he could do now but accept the fact that most of the money he had was spent on car that broke down.

"At least I still have $500," he thought. He wondered if there was any way he could purchase another vehicle with that money but being realistically he knew a car at that price would surely have the same reliability as his first car. Then, he remembered what his dad had told him earlier that day before handing him the money. He remembered how his dad had given him the option to multiply it. But how was he going to do that? Johnny then took out his cell phone and began to browse the internet for ideas on how he could double his money. He clicked on the first article that read, "Five ways to multiply your money," and delve right into it. The first option was to invest in real estate, but he knew he didn't have enough money to begin with. He read idea after idea until he came across the option that really captured his curiosity. It was of course learning how to invest in the stock market. He had heard of this before but didn't know how to go about it. He then thought it'd be a great idea to go to the bookstore and purchase a beginner's book on investing in the stock market.

Once he had the book in his possession, Johnny read and reread that book until he understood everything. Once he understood everything about the basics, he reached out to one of his friend's dad that had some experience with the stock market. His friend's dad helped Johnny set up a brokerage account with the remaining $500 he had and informed him about which company stocks to be on the lookout for. With everything that Johnny had learned from his book and the experience of his friend's dad, he slowly began making profit with every trade. Within three months of continuously trading, he was able to amount a whopping $27,000. His father was very proud of the lesson Johnny had learned. He knew his son was never going to have financial problems ever again.

When it came time to return back to the dealership, Johnny was happy to know his next purchase wasn't going to end up like his first.

4. Guard Your Money. Don't Lose It.

The money you have saved is bound to be lost should you use it wrongly. Handle your money in a way that will not jeopardize it and instead preserve it. If there is a less expensive option with the same quality as a more expensive one, opt for the lesser. If you learn to protect your money, it will stay with you unlike the man that doesn't guard his money. Do not reach into your accumulated wealth as it will slowly start to leak empty over time.

5. Ask Questions To Those Who Are Experienced, Not Ones Who Aren't Successful.

It is not wise to ask guidance from those that have not done it before. There was a man that wanted to learn how to create passive income because he was tired of not having a luxurious lifestyle. He had spent most of his life working as a blacksmith for the village leader and didn't want to spend the rest of his life doing it. Someone had given him the advice to save up a good amount of money and then invest it. So that's exactly what he did. The blacksmith worked hard every single day for an entire year before he was able to save up a good deal of money. Now that he had acquired a good sum of money, he had to think about what he wanted to do with it. He knew he wanted to make more money, but the ideas were just not coming to him.

That day, the man's older brother, who was a bricklayer, had arrived into town to visit him. The man still could not come up with any ideas so he decided to ask his brother for guidance on how he should invest his money. His brother told him that he knew a man that became one of the wealthiest man in his village by selling jewelry made from gold. The blacksmith heard his brother and thought this was a grand idea. He thought, if he could purchase golden jewelry and sell it at a higher price, he'd become wealthy in no time. "Introduce me to this wealthy man you speak of brother. I have many questions to ask him." The blacksmith said. "If it's answers you want, look no further than me. I have seen how this man has acquired his wealth and won't need seek him out for you. I will show you how he did it." his older brother said. The man then entrusted his brother with his one years' worth of savings and asked him to go to the jewelry market in the next town over and purchase as much jewelry as he could for him. Rumors were there was a jewelry market that sold some of the most beautiful jewelry anyone has ever seen.

  The man was so thankful his brother was willing to go for him because he himself had to finish a job the village leader had given him. After receiving the money, the man's brother journeyed 45 miles by horse to the next town in order to purchase as much jewelry as he could. Once he arrived at the market, he was greeted by many beautiful women that offered him a discount on all of their jewelry. The women told him every piece of jewelry was made with real gold and would sell for twice the amount anywhere else. Hearing this, the man's brother believed the woman and purchased every piece of jewelry he could with his brother's savings. Later that day, he packed the horse and returned to his brother's village to deliver the jewelry.

  Upon arrival, the blacksmith walked out of his home and welcomed back his older brother. Right behind him, another man had walked out of his home. The blacksmith introduced the mysterious man to his older brother as an experienced jewelry maker. The blacksmith had invited him over in order to inspect the jewelry and advise him on selling it. After they shook hands, the blacksmith's older brother carefully unloaded the horse and laid out a tarp on the ground and placed the jewelry on top of it. "Heavens. Where did you say you bought this jewelry from?" the experienced old man said. "The jewelry market in the next town over. Why do you ask?" the blacksmith's brother said. "I fear you have been lied to. This jewelry is made out of fool's gold."

If you seek to become a millionaire, do not ask a non-millionaire for advice.

6. Own Your Home.

There are times it is important to rent, and there are times it is important to own. In the case of housing, it is very important you own your home. Shelter is imperative to one's survival as it is one of our basic human necessities. Take that away and our chances diminish. In order to secure the future survivability of your family, one must plan to own his home. If you are renting your shelter, no matter how many payments or how much it costs you to continue living there, you will never amass any equity. After five years of living there, not only will you not own any part of your home, but you would only be accumulating wealth for the actual owner of the house who's renting it to you. Own your home.

7. Provide For Your Future Self And Family.

Strategize your decisions based on the future. It is your responsibility to create a stable foundation on which your family will be supported for generations to come. As you've just read, completely owning your home will allow mortgage-free shelter for your family in the future. The idea here is to set yourself and your family up for a future where liabilities will siphon less of the wealth you have accumulated. By protecting your wealth, properly investing it into assets, and teaching your family the importance of doing so, there will be much prosperity for generations to come even after your death. There will come a day when the sands of your hourglass will run out and every business and asset you have will either continue to provide and flourish or collapse and return your family back into the Rat Race.

8. The More You Learn, The More You Earn.

If you don't know how to do something, simply pick up a book on the topic and read it. You have to view each book as a treasure chest. Inside every single book is a hidden golden nugget of wisdom or advice that can be revolutionary if applied correctly to your life. Seek mentors as they will be your opportunity to close the knowledge gap. The more knowledge you have about acquiring wealth, the sooner you will have it

9. Do Not Purchase That For Which You Are Unable To Pay.

We buy luxuries because we want impress the people around us. We do this by creating a facade in order to present ourselves as wealthy and powerful. This can be extremely dangerous as it can cause a major setback on your journey to become financially free. For example, so many people are set on buying a brand-new sports car or boat to show off to their friends and colleagues yet end up finding themselves in a financial struggle trying to come up with high monthly payments.

10. Have Compassion For Those Who Have Been Crippled By Misfortune And Aid Them Within Reasonable Limits.

Those of us with a big heart wish we could help everyone less fortunate. There's something about pulling up next to homeless man or woman on the side of the street that makes us wish life would just give them another chance. But the situation we find ourselves in most is seeing the people we care about whether they be your friends or family struggle financially. For example, your parents. As their son or daughter, you feel obligated to give them every handout they need because it feels like you owe it to them for bringing you into this world. It's understandable. We hate to see the people we care about most struggle. It's normal to feel this way, and I encourage you to help. Just don't give too much to the point where you find yourself struggling financially as well. There is nothing wrong with giving handouts and helping people you care about, just keep it within reasonable means. Do not allow yourself to become a victim of those who only wish to mooch off you. Be wary of leeches.

11. Take Advantage Of A Good Opportunity.

There was man named Cairo that traveled from town to town selling homemade quilts. His routine would consist of traveling into one town, setting up near the local market to sell as many quilts as he could before packing up and leaving. It had already been two days since he last set foot in the previous town. The route Cairo was taking expected him to arrive at the next town within three days. He knew he wasn't that far from the town as the third day was now coming to its end. The sun had set, but the sky was still lit with warm colors. Night was slowly approaching.

As Cairo kept walking down the dirt path through the woods, he could see something odd blocking the pathway in the distance. He didn't know what it was but could tell the structure was made out of wood. This seemed strange to Cairo, but he kept walking anyway seeing as how it was the only path available at the time. Eventually, Cairo got close enough to the structure that he was finally able to identify what it was. A bridge! And underneath it? A large ravine that stretched as far as the eye could see in either direction. Clearly the bridge was the only way to get across, but it had been propped in the up position from the opposite side. Cairo knew there was no way him and his horse could get across without using that bridge. His only option was to spend the night on the path until the bridge had been lowered by one of the townspeople in the morning.

As Cairo was finishing setting up his campsite, he began to hear a rumbling noise coming from behind him. The noise sounded very distinctive. It was as if it were a herd of animals heading in his direction up the path. As the noise increasingly got louder and closer, in the distance Cairo could now see that it was indeed a herd of about twenty cattle and with it was a small group of three men shepherding it. Cairo introduced himself when he met face to face with the group's leader, Audemars, and asked them what had brought them along the path as well. Audemars told Cairo that they were cattle salesman traveling from town to town. Knowing he was in the presence of a fellow salesman, Cairo smiled and introduced himself as quilt salesman who also traveled from town to town. "I see the bridge is up. Let us join or friend Cairo tonight and wait for the bridge to be lowered in the morning." Audemars said to the other men.

That night, temperatures began to drop more than usual. As Cairo got colder, he decided to use one of the many quilts he had to keep himself warm. He stood up and walked over to his horse and removed one of the quilts. He wrapped it around himself and walked back to the campfire. Audemars and his freezing men saw that Cairo had returned with one of his quilts and decided to ask him if he was willing to barter for his quilts. At least that way Audemars and his men wouldn't freeze to death before they were able to make it to the next town. Audemars turned to Cairo and proposed a barter. He was willing to give Cairo his twenty livestock in exchange for eight quilts. Cairo did the math and calculated it was an even trade but was hasty. Although he would still have a few quilts left over and wouldn't be losing any money doing the barter, he wasn't experienced selling cattle and didn't want to jeopardize his earnings in the next town. Kindly, Cairo declined the offer as he explained he didn't have any experience shepherding or selling cattle. Audemars heard what Cairo had to say and accepted his decision not to barter with him. Audemars and his men decided instead to gather the cattle and surround themselves with them in order to produce enough warmth to get them through the night. The night was very cold, but they managed.

    The next morning, Cairo, Audemars and his men were awoken to a loud creaking noise. To their liking, it was the bridge itself being lowered. Once the bridge was in place, to their surprise, an enormous crowd appeared on the other side of the bridge and began to walk across. When they reached the other side, they identified themselves as residents from the town ahead. They had ventured out early in the morning to capture animals because their meat supply had been infested by rodents. All of their meat had been tainted and the town was left with no meat to sell or eat. One of the residents from the back of the crowd saw the cattle asked if any of the cattle were up for sale. The man said he was willing to pay top dollar for three of those cattle because his daughter's wedding was tomorrow and the main course was going to be meat. Soon after, most of the crowd began to offer their money in exchange for a chance to purchase one of the livestock. Audemars looked back at his men with a smile stretching from cheek to cheek because an idea had occurred to him. He turned back to face the crowd and with a loud voice he put his cattle up for sale at price three times their worth. One by one the townspeople paid Audemars the hefty price in exchange for his livestock. And when there were no more to sell, Audemars and his men had made enough money to purchase anything their hearts desired.

Don't pass on an opportunity to learn. Even if you don't have any experience. Say yes, then figure it out as you go.

12. Money Flows To The Solution.

Do not chase money, as you will never catch up to it. The only way to make money willingly flow into your pocket is by solving a problem. Think about the many problems you encounter in your everyday life. You are probably not the only one encountering this problem. Think about ways to resolve them. People will pay for the solution.

The Phoenix

If you have a dream, you have to protect it. People don't believe they can do something great themselves, so they'll go and tell you you can't either. If you truly want something, go get it. Period. The worst thing you can do is quit throughout the journey. I've quit before. I've quit because it hurt. I couldn't bear continuing to work towards my dreams and not seeing any results. The pain radiated throughout my heart and soul to the point where I had enough. I felt as if there was no way it could get any worse. I felt there was no way I could come back. I felt there was no way I could fix it.

Listen to me. No matter the distance; keep moving forward. No matter the time it takes to complete; keep moving forward. No matter the pain; keep moving forward. Pain is temporary. Pain may last an hour, a day, a month, or even a year, but eventually it will subside. What will take the place of pain is happiness and success. If you quit however, that pain will last forever.

Read what I am about to tell you, and after you are finished, I want you to close your eyes and imagine it. I want you to imagine a tall hefty man with a dark bearded face. This man wears a black apron around his shop and has soot smudged all over his clothes and body. Slowly, he pours a cast iron cauldron filled with hot melted metal over a blackened template. Once the metal has been cooled, the man picks up and raises the template over his head and with all his might he slams and smashes the template on the ground. The template shatters into many pieces and the only thing left is a metal sheath. The man then places the metal sheath on top of his anvil and proceeds to hit it as hard as he can with a heavy hammer.

This is life. Life is a blacksmith.

You were brought into this world innocent. You did not know fear, nor pain. But as you grew, life's simplicities began to fade. You began to work for your money and because of that you felt trapped and miserable. You knew deep down you weren't being paid what you were actually worth but paid enough to keep crawling back to your job. Eventually you realized the only way to get out of the Rat Race was to figure out a way to make more money. You sat down in a chair and scribbled some notes on a piece of paper until you thought of an idea you were almost certain would work. So, you put it to the test. Although you had set all your pawns in the right place, it didn't go the way you had hoped. Then you tried again only to repeat the same outcome. Struggle after struggle. Setback after setback. It felt as if there was no point in trying to escape anymore because of the countless failures. Something always had to get in the way. Soon, you began to question why God had cursed you to live trial after trial with no hope of improvement. You became overwhelmed with the weight of life on your shoulders. Feeling stuck and not knowing what to do, you took the easy way out. You quit. You threw in the towel. All because of pain. But I'm here to inform you that this is necessary. Pain is necessary. You see, when the blacksmith placed the metal sheath on the anvil and began to hammer it as hard he could, he did not do this out of hate for the sword In truth, he did this in order to forge and fortify it so that it would not shatter into pieces the moment it was used in battle. You need to view your pain this way. Pain is not your enemy. Pain is one of life's best teachers. Some of the best lessons in life are learned from pain.

Life is a blacksmith, you are the sword, and pain is the hammer. When life continues to hammer you down, remember that it is necessary in order to strengthen your will. Life hammers you with pain in order to forge you and fortify your will so that it doesn't break easily along your journey.

So, the next time life has you up against the ropes and you've depleted everything you have. When you've run out of energy. When you've run out of patience. When you've run out hope. Dig deep down. Dig deep down and muster up every ounce of energy you have left to **KEEP MOVING FORWARD.** You will be tested. You will fall, but you must rise. No matter how many times your face has been pushed into the dirt, place your hands on the ground firmly and push yourself up once more. Never give up. You are better than that. You are stronger than that. You are a champion. Believe in this deep down in your heart. You are enough. You can do it. Forget what everyone else has told you up to this point. Stop doubting yourself. Enough is enough. You need to start fighting back. Get up and go after it. If you need to crawl, fine. That's acceptable. Falling is acceptable. Crying is acceptable. Puking is acceptable. Bleeding is acceptable. What isn't acceptable is quitting.

Think about all the people in your life right now that are looking up to you. You may be their only hope. Do it for them if you have to. Think about all the people that want nothing more than to see you never accomplish your goals. The best revenge is major success so go out there and do it. Believe in yourself even when others don't. Even if you still don't believe in yourself, I don't care, just make sure you do this for the ones who are counting on you. Armor your will as much as possible because life is going to throw everything it can at you. Resist the temptation to quit. Plant your feet on the dirt firmly and stand your ground. Be **TENACIOUS.** I know you were meant to do great things. Even if somehow you still don't believe in yourself, just know I believe in you. The moment you decided to pick up this book and change your destiny, I believed in you. I've always believed in you.

You picked up this book with hopes of finding the answers when in reality the keys to your freedom have always been in your pocket. All I did was remind you they were there.

Do Me A Favor

Thank you for purchasing this book and supporting it. I'm confident you're well on your way to accomplish great things and gain your freedom. Please gift this book to everyone you think needs to read it. Post about this book anywhere and everywhere so people will see and buy it. Please take a moment to write a great review and five-star it on Amazon. Reviews are the best way for independent authors like myself to get noticed and sell more books. I also read every review and use the feedback to write future revisions and future books.

Thank you from the bottom of my heart.

- Carlos Bermudez

Proof

Made in the USA
Columbia, SC
28 July 2018